BUT FIRST, *dream* BIGGER

BUT FIRST, dream BIGGER

How to Unlock Your Potential and Find Your True Calling in 21 Days

by

NADIA MAU BERNARDY

Copyright © 2023 by Nadia Mau Bernardy

Published in the United States by eBooks2go, Inc.
1827 Walden Office Square, Suite 260, Schaumburg, IL 60173

Cover Photo Credit:
Juliana Offergeld Photography
Gifted by Lindsay Johnson

Author Photo credit:
Emma Whitney Photography

All rights reserved. No part of this book may be reproduced by any mechanical, photographic, or electronic process.

The author of this book does not dispense medical advice or prescribe the use of any technique as a form of treatment.

1st Edition 2023

Printed in the United States of America

ISBN: 978-1-5457-5674-4

Nadia Mau Bernardy
375 West Kuiaha Unit 23
Haiku, HI 96708
www.nadiabernardy.com

Quantity Purchases:
Companies, professional groups, clubs, and other organizations may qualify for special terms when ordering quantities of this title.
For information, email info@ebooks2go.net,
or call (847) 598-1150 ext. 4141.
www.ebooks2go.net

Library of Congress Cataloging in Publication

To my mother, MaxFran,
who taught me the true power of
your mind and what it means to dream BIGGER.

Contents

Preface ix
Introduction xiii

Day 1 1
Day 2 5
Day 3 15
Day 4 19
Day 5 23
Day 6 27
Day 7 37
Day 8 41
Day 9 45
Day 10 55
Day 11 61
Day 12 67
Day 13 77
Day 14 81
Day 15 89
Day 16 93
Day 17 99
Day 18 103
Day 19 107

Day 20 109
Day 21 113

Acknowledgements 127
Testimonials 129
Offerings and Resources 131
Affiliates and Product Suggestions 133
About the author 135

Preface

The Power of Your Mind

My grandmother once said if my mother were stranded in the desert, a limousine would suddenly appear out of nowhere and take her exactly where she needed to go. My mother had this incredible way of tapping into her subconscious mind even when things seemed bleak.

Shortly after I was born, she was diagnosed with brain, breast, and lymphoma cancer. The doctors gave her seven years to live. She had other plans—to beat the odds stacked so highly against her and to live her dream life in Hawaii for the next 21 years.

This is the power of your subconscious mind—you decide. Many members of society believe they are operating from their conscious minds. However, it is our subconscious minds that determine everything in our lives. You have this incredible power within you, and the sooner you realize this, the sooner you can transition into a life that reflects what you truly desire.

My mother was one of the purest people I ever knew. She could change her reality through positive thinking like no one I had ever met. She always told me I could create my desired life if I genuinely embodied my dreams.

And now I am here to tell you the same. Your economic status, social and professional network and daily struggles do not matter. What matters is that you truly believe life is not out of your control—you are in control. I understand it does not always feel that way; sometimes, we want to run away and cry. But, even if things are not how you desire them to be, this is just an opportunity to design them the way you want them to be. And this is why I wrote this book. To help guide you toward that first desire, that dream that is 100 percent attainable in 21 days so you can see your power and understand what is possible.

Growing up, I always had a clear vision of the life I wanted to live. However, as I got older, the outside world did an excellent job of reminding me of my limitations. Being raised by a single mother comes with its own set of preconceived stereotypes. It was as if not having a father figure meant I was forever damaged and would never amount to anything. While I see the benefits of being raised in a two-parent household, that does not determine that you will be an outstanding citizen. We all know examples where people have excelled and failed in both scenarios.

However, my mother always reminded me that I could achieve anything I wanted. She ensured that I went to a private Catholic school for most of my life; she always encouraged me to enter the school talent shows, challenged me to be as creative as possible with my art projects, and had me try out for any sport I was interested in.

I didn't realize it then, but she instilled confidence in me and set a solid foundation for what I would accomplish later in life. It was because of my mother that I believed I could try out for anything and excel despite the opinions or doubts of others. This foundation served me well when I went to art school in Albuquerque, New Mexico, to study graphic design, web design, and marketing.

If you have ever studied art, you know that class critiques can be brutal. I remember spending hours agonizing over a campaign for a local shoe store called Ruby Shoesday. Even though it was simply a school project, I treated it as if the store's owner would use my designs. I came up with what I thought was a very dynamic campaign. I even showed it to friends outside of school, and everyone seemed to love it. But when it was time to present, the entire class, including my professor, ripped it to shreds. I had to start all over from scratch.

It was times like these when it would have been so easy for me to give up. Trust me when I say critiques exactly like that cause so many people to drop out of art school. But I sacrificed so much to be there. I moved away from my island home, away from my friends, and was apart from my mother for the first time. Giving up was not an option. Instead, I used the critique to fuel me into creating an even better design. I did not allow the opinions of others to dictate my ability to create a phenomenal piece.

Many situations like this one caused me to pause and question my potential. But, ultimately, I knew what was possible for me. If it is possible for me—a Maui girl raised by a single mother who beat incredible odds—to create her dreams, then it is possible for you too.

Introduction

But First, Dream Bigger

In 2011, I was hired to work at an unknown tech startup in San Francisco. I lived in Albuquerque, New Mexico, and was laid off from my first real job after college. The company was going under and could no longer afford to pay for the marketing manager position they had created for me. I was intrigued when I heard about this new company that would revolutionize how we traveled.

The company flew me out to San Francisco for training. I was wide-eyed and ready for something new. The week before Halloween was my favorite time of year, and excitement was in the air. I stayed in a quintessential San Francisco apartment in North Beach. I was so excited that I took the first flight to roam around the city. I hadn't visited to see my father since I was about nine years old.

I had a strong sense that, even though I had no idea what to expect, I was exactly where I was meant to be. During that first week of training, I learned that the company was launched to meet a need for more places to stay. There was a design conference in San Francisco, and all the hotels were booked. The company's founders decided to rent out their air mattresses to great success, and Airbnb was born. After this initial win, the founders faced many challenges before Airbnb became a household name. Despite these perceived failures, the company became a major disruptor in the travel space.

It was incredible how an inspired idea turned into something bigger. We all have the potential to tap into an idea and make it a reality. Not too long after getting hired as a remote employee for Airbnb, I realized

I could live anywhere. In March of 2012, I moved back home to Maui with my fiancé, now husband. I could not have imagined that taking this job would lead me down the path to creating the life I had dreamed of since I was 16. I had a vision for the life I desired and took aligned action on the opportunities as they presented themselves, especially if they felt incredibly risky and bold.

We tend to want to avoid risk at all costs, but if you get quiet and listen, your intuition knows the way. We have been trained over time to listen to external forces instead of trusting our inner guidance. This book invites you to take action on the dream tapping you on the shoulder.

Throughout this intuitive 21-day guide, I will first teach you how to connect to your soul calling by uncovering your Soulfulpreneur Archetype. Everything starts with you first. Before you can genuinely relate to your dream, we need to discover your soul-led story, your legacy, and your path in life.

Once we uncover the foundation, it is time to connect to your dream through the Dream Bigger Exercise, Visionary Board Exercise, and work through your Inspired Ideas.

We will then move on to taking aligned action. Once you have clarity, it is time to make a long-term plan, create rituals, and focus on what I like to call your Creative Windows of time.

This intuitive 21-day guide will take you from feeling called to start to giving you powerful insights to move you forward.

This book is perfect for you if you have that unsettled feeling that you are supposed to be doing something but are not doing it. You have an idea of a dream, a calling, that you have been thinking about taking action on for weeks, months, or even years. You feel like something is missing in your life, and you need support with connecting the dots. This dream you feel called to start could be learning how to paint, finally writing that book, speaking on stage, starting your business, or taking that trip to Greece. No matter what that calling is, remember that you are here to take action on it and dream BIGGER.

You Are Here to Dream Bigger

Day 1

But First, Dream Bigger

21 days to your true calling

I first decided I wanted to work online from home in Hawaii when I was 16 years old. The Internet entrepreneur was barely even a thing, social media did not exist, and I had no idea how I was going to make this dream my reality.

I simply knew that I wanted to be able to stay home with my kids while also having a career. I was always so grateful that my mother was home when I got home from school, and I wanted the same for my kids. I had no idea what that meant or what career I could have, but anything and everything felt possible. I was setting myself up to thrive on what would be the future of work in the online space.

I always knew I was meant to do something creative that I loved.

Fast forward to today, and I am all about the laptop lifestyle. Honestly, I've been working online from home for so long, since 2011, I couldn't even imagine returning to an office. It was my dream to move back home to Maui and work online, and if I can create my dream life, then you can too. There is no limit to what you can achieve, and it can be done using the skills and knowledge you already have.

Especially after 2020, working from home and online is no longer seen as a "utopian" idea by most people. It is the current state of the world; thank you, Internet. There has never been another time like this, and your time is NOW. Take this opportunity, and create the life you want doing the work that LIGHTS you up!

If you could take action on any dream, what would you do? What would you create? Where would you go? Who would you go there with?

But First, Dream Bigger

Exercise

When I think about dreaming bigger, the word "audacious" comes to mind. It's the grand, out-of-this-world dream that you can hardly imagine coming true. While audacious dreams are exciting, remember that dreams are made on the other side of taking daily aligned action. I think many of us believe that dreams will come true without little action. Don't get me wrong. Miracles are real; we see them every day. But in most cases, making your dreams a reality requires you to first believe in them and then take daily action. The action will always be one you can take, and this book is meant to guide you toward bridging the gap between where you are now and where you want to go. You can use this guide for as many dreams as you wish. To begin, I recommend starting simple with a dream you really identify with. Then, as the smaller dreams start to take shape, go with bigger and bigger ones. Each manifestation will prove that you have the power to create anything you want in your mind.

To help you connect to the dream you will create in the next 21 days, I want to share a simple exercise to get started. Have you ever heard of a brain dump? It is the practice of getting out a piece of paper and writing down everything that comes to mind. I usually do this with coaching clients when they have many ideas and need help figuring out which one to move forward on. While it works for airing out your thoughts, it also helps to narrow a list down to your dreams.

Most of us have more than one dream to bring to life. Our plans range from wanting to start a business to learning how to make pasta from scratch to dreaming of flying a plane. Learning to fly a plane is one of my husband's biggest dreams so that we can easily travel interisland. I can't wait for this one to manifest.

Each one of your dreams is just as important as the rest. However, we often get so overwhelmed by which dream to take action on first that we never move forward with them. That is why getting all your dreams, no matter the category, out of your head and down on paper is essential.

I invite you to get your favorite journal or a piece of paper and dream dump your ideas. Before you say you don't know what to write or only have one, I encourage you to clear your mind briefly.

Find a quiet spot outside or somewhere in your home and sit still. Allow yourself to calm your breath. Be aware of the sounds around you and pay attention to the thoughts coming to mind. Try not to judge them if they seem all over the place. It's okay to think about what you want to make for dinner or that phone call you need to make that you've been putting off; pay attention to the thoughts that are naturally coming to you.

After sitting quietly for three to five minutes, I will give you a simple journal prompt.

If I could have any of my dreams come true without anything getting in the way, what would they be?

You should make a list of 21 dreams, big and small. If you end up with more, great, and if you can't make it to 21, don't force yourself. Just make sure you have something to work with.

Now that you have your list, circle the top ten dreams you want to bring to life in the next 21 days. From the ten dreams, put a star next to the top five dreams. Then look at the five dreams and honestly ask yourself which goal you can start taking action on in the next 21 days without putting anything in the way.

Which dream stuck out to you most? Write that one down again in your journal or on a piece of paper. This is the dream you are going to focus on. Before you start questioning whether this is the right dream, I want to remind you that your initial feeling is intuition.

Now that you have selected your dream, we will run it through a filter. I like to refer to it as your soul-led filter. This will help you connect your vision back to yourself and the skills you already have to bring this dream to life. In addition, it will provide you with the path you need to take and confirm that this dream is the right one for you to take action on in the next 21 days.

Dream Outside the Box
Day 1 Journal Prompts

Make space for your dreams today and watch as they unfold.

Somewhere along the way, we stopped dreaming bigger. We settled with what we had and stopped believing in magic. But that time has come to an end. It is time to Dream BIGGER again.

What dream did you put on the back burner?

What inspired idea has been tapping you on the shoulder?

What aligned action can you take today?

What simple step is right in front of you?

What Is Your Soul Calling You to Do?

Day 2

Uncover Your Soul Calling

Do you know who your soul is calling you to be?

I often wonder why I started my spiritual-awakening journey so late in life. I lost both of my parents in my mid-20s, two years apart, and one would think this would catapult me into spirituality. But it didn't. At the time, I was focused on graduating from college and starting my career. Looking back, it was almost like I pushed grieving aside to stay on track. I numbed myself with my ambition and just powered through.

It wasn't until after I had my daughter, at the age of 30, that I started to feel that change. After that, I started to feel like something was shifting in me, and I was experimenting with all of the endless possibilities.

In 2017, this chapter of my life went from dreamy fun and experimenting to stuck, lost, confused, and this unsettled feeling of longing. I started to feel very clearly that I was supposed to be doing something, but I wasn't doing it.

The problem was I needed help figuring out what this something was. Do you ever feel like that? Do you feel like that now?

I feel embarrassed sharing this because, with all the time I spent dreaming up ideas, I could have just taken action on at least one, like my husband suggested, but I just couldn't.

I started to feel like something was wrong with me. So I went to see a therapist for the first time. I thought talking to someone who didn't know me personally would help. I felt a neutral perspective would give me greater insight into the answers I so desperately sought.

Therapy was the most-awkward experience for me, and I remember during my first session asking how it was all supposed to work, which I'm guessing the therapist hears a lot.

The first few sessions were helpful. I started to see where I was holding onto things from my past that kept me in a loop. I began to understand how I persevere through things without giving myself a break.

The biggest realization was that I valued hard work and the hustle mentality over rest, relaxation, and giving back to myself, a.k.a. self-care and self-love.

I thought because I was working online from home in tech while helping clients build their dreams in my side hustle business, I had a work–life balance figured out. But what I had was the complete opposite. I was working, working, working without giving myself time and space to relax.

And that's when I had the most significant realization: I could never move forward with any of my ideas because I was not giving them time and space to breathe and to allow them to flourish.

It was almost like I was planting the seed, and as the sprout started to emerge from the soil, instead of watering it, I was giving the water to my laptop, clients, friends, and family, and I was completely neglecting myself and my idea. So the idea would die, and then a new one would form, but the cycle would repeat itself.

It may seem obvious, or this gives you some realization about your ideas and dreams. But it was an important breakthrough for me to realize that I had to give them the honored attention they deserved for my ideas to grow.

I needed to create space and time for them, which meant I needed to give myself time and space and take a pause from anything else that was getting in the way or distracting me.

I know this can be easier said than done, as we live in a world where constant distractions are pulling us in every other direction. But it is necessary. We must create the space—something I like to refer to as sacred space—every single day to focus on our ideas to help make them a reality.

In this book, I will guide you through creating this space so that you can find clarity, pick your one idea, and start taking daily aligned action on it to bring your dream to life.

One particular therapy session was incredibly enlightening for me. When I told my therapist about all my ideas and that I couldn't seem to bring anything to life or move past the beginning stage, she asked me a straightforward question: "When was the last time you took time off?"

I stopped for a moment because working online from home and traveling, I never really felt like I needed to take time off. I felt like I had this beautiful work–life balance that allowed me so much space and time. The problem was I was not taking this space and time. In all available moments, if I was not working, I cared for my daughter. If I was not caring for my daughter, I was running my side business with my husband. If I was not doing that, I was working.

There was no space. I was not creating space. I was using all available space to work and constantly stay busy. While the hustle mentality is celebrated in the United States, there is a better way. A way that allows you to give back to yourself, to others and your work, and is called flow.

Flow allows you to create that sacred space, taking daily aligned action to give back to yourself and others. But it has to be intentional. It has to be honored, respected, and encouraged. You cannot neglect this flow—sacred space—you need to focus on it. And when you do this, things will start to fall into place.

After thinking, I finally responded to my therapist, "Well, I took time off to get married, and I took time off to have a baby. But that wasn't really time off."

She said, "Right. When was the last time you took time off to have fun?"

I paused again and replied, "Well, we went to New Zealand as a family, and it was really fun, but I wouldn't say it was relaxing. We road-tripped around the North island the entire trip, went surfing, stayed with friends, and were in constant motion. I usually take a few days off when I travel for work or for our business to enjoy the city we are in, but it is not strictly for fun because it's ultimately a work trip."

She looked at me peacefully and said, "What about taking time off just for you to recharge and refresh?"

I almost fell off my chair. Do people do that? I thought. It was such a strange and foreign concept to me.

At this point, you are most likely in two camps: You can either totally relate, as you have never taken time off to rest either, or you think I am absolutely nuts, as self-care is a consistent part of your life. If you are in the first camp, this book will help you create the space and infuse more self-care and rest into your life. It will also allow you to amplify your efforts using what I call work and woo modes. More on that later.

But if you are already taking time for yourself, this book will help you elevate this process even more and work with your current routine. If you are in the second camp, let me just say I admire your respect for rest.

I finally replied, "I've never really taken time off to rest."

"Nadia!" she replied, almost as stunned as I was that people rest. "You will not be able to bring your ideas to life if you are not taking time off to rest and give back to yourself. This is why you are stuck and unable to move forward. There is nowhere for your ideas to living, breathe, and come alive."

It made total sense, but I had never considered it. The whole time I was trying to create with zero space to create. Now looking back, it seems obvious. Why didn't I see this before?

We get so into our habits, routines, and patterns and so busy with life that we often miss what is right in front of us. We also believe that because everything is go, go, go, we are supposed to create this way. That everything is moving so fast that we can't possibly stop to create. Everything is happening all at once, and if we pause, we will miss out. Life is so busy there is no time to stop.

But stopping is necessary to allow the ideas to flow, inspiration to happen, and the aligned action to occur. How do you expect to create anything if you are so exhausted from life?

When my therapist said I needed to take time off from work to rest, I replied, "Okay, I'll look into when I can make that happen."

"Oh no," she replied, "this needs to happen immediately. You are on the verge of a nervous breakdown. You cannot go on another day this way."

It was a pivotal moment for me because, as adults, we are so used to making our own decisions. We go through life in a way we think is best. We rarely stop to ask others what they believe or to get advice. At that moment, I felt like a child who was taking direction in a way I hadn't done in years. But I knew it was in my best interest.

"Okay," I replied. "I will talk to my manager on Monday."

I am manifesting three months of paid time off.

On Monday, I reached out to my manager. She was my sixth lead in the almost seven years I had worked for Airbnb. Before being on her team, I was on what I call the dream team. My colleagues from this team and I are still friends to this day. We worked so well together that we repeatedly hit records, won "Air Awards," as they were called, and genuinely loved working together. This was a time during my career at Airbnb when everything felt right. I was living the dream, working for my dream company, and working my dream job with my dream team.

Then my lead got a promotion, and our mighty dream team merged into another team. They did things differently than us, and while my old lead gave us a lot of autonomy to do our work, which was why we excelled, my new lead did not. As a remote team, our new lead had a lot of trust issues and was constantly paranoid that we weren't working. This led to ridiculous rules and low morale.

When I joined this team, I was extremely proud of the work I was doing for the business travel project. It was a new initiative to get more companies to think of Airbnb while traveling. I also worked on a collaboration with the Make-A-Wish Foundation, helping a young boy with cancer come to Maui to go zip-lining.

I was on this career high, and that all came crashing down once our team merged. We quickly nicknamed ourselves the "dumping ground," and our work and the meaning behind our work just stopped making sense. We worked on random projects from all different departments with no rhyme or reason. It was almost like our new lead was trying to prove that we were relevant and productive so that we could stay remote.

You see, even though you might think working remotely for a company like Airbnb made total sense, as the company grew, there became more and more pressure to join the mothership, as we called it, and relocate to the main office, which was either Portland, Oregon (my home office) or the headquarters (HQ) in San Francisco, California.

I almost moved several times, especially when my beloved business travel project could only be done from HQ in San Francisco. But I dreamed of living in Maui and working from home, so I just tried to persevere through it.

Things got more intense as time passed, and I needed a break, but we were always busy. So I never asked.

When I finally requested time off, my lead quickly gave it to me. I had never taken an extended leave of absence before and was relieved by how easy the process was.

I started filling out the forms to take three months off unpaid personal leave starting that next week when the company made an unexpected announcement.

To say that the hustle mentality was celebrated at Airbnb was an understatement. After all the incredible growth and milestones we reached over the almost seven years I had worked there, including all the hard work, sleepless nights, and traveling away from our families, the company realized it was time for us to rest. Airbnb was now a $32 billion company, an acronym written into pop songs, and here to stay.

We all deserved to rest.

Two days after requesting my leave of absence, a new program was announced: the "Recharge and Refresh Program," in which you could take paid time off to chill. I didn't think twice and asked how to start that process. The program wasn't official yet, so I had to postpone my leave by two weeks.

I was the first employee to apply for the Recharge and Refresh Program. The recharge team was excited to see how much it was needed and to help me be the first person in the company to take it. I have to note, at this time, in the summer of 2017, there were almost 357,899 Airbnb employees and 34 offices in 345 countries around the world, plus those of us still working remotely. To give some perspective, I was the 51st employee ever hired, and there was only one small office.

When I returned to my therapist that Friday to tell her about the new Recharge and Refresh Program, she almost fell off her chair. She spoke a sentence that still sits with me today: "Wow, Nadia, the universe answered you in a big way!"

She then advised me to use my time off to truly rest. I had to resist the urge to make big plans or create endless ideas for creative projects. At first, I found it extremely difficult to unwind, but as the days went on, I slowly began to relax.

I started to go on soul dates in the forest. I would wander around, listening to the trees blow in the wind. Olinda Forest in Makawao Town, where I grew up, was my favorite place to go.

On one particular day, about a month into my time off, I had an unusual experience. It was a typical day. I first dropped my daughter off at preschool and headed up to the forest like I had several times before during my time off.

I pulled into the parking lot. There were a few other cars, but it wasn't too busy. I began walking down the trail as the wind picked up. It was a beautiful morning. Slightly cool but with sunshine peeking through the trees.

Not too far along the path, I noticed an older woman who appeared to be her young caregiver sitting on a tree log. The birds were chirping. The wind was slightly blowing. I could hear the branches creaking just a little bit. The wind almost sounded like water running down a stream. I smiled at the women slightly, but they seemed engaged in a conversation.

I took only a few steps past the women who were sitting on my left-hand side when everything stopped. The wind was quiet, the trees stood perfectly still, and I could not hear the birds.

What happened next was something I had never experienced before. The best way I can describe it was that I floated above my body into the forest. I felt light as air. Even though I was up in the trees, I didn't feel scared. Everything felt very calm. Then I was imprinted with a profound thought I had never had before. Everything in my life was happening in response to me. Life was not happening to me. I created my reality.

Before I knew it was back in my body, the wind picked up again, all the birds were chirping, and the branches were in motion. I took a few steps forward. I looked up only to see the older woman and her caregiver walking toward me. I don't remember them passing me. I immediately felt that those few moments had been a lot longer.

I decided to go home. I pulled into my driveway, sat on my couch, and it kicked in. The life that I was living was the exact life I told myself I was going to live when I was sixteen years old. I did more than just set some goals and reach them. I created every single aspect of the life I was currently living. I was living in the town I told myself I would live in, in the type of house I said I would have, working my dream job online for Airbnb, married to my husband, and raising our daughter together. It was as I had dreamed of, down to the last detail.

This out-of-body experience was the catapult for my spiritual awakening. It helped me to realize that we live in a society that does not encourage us to connect to our inner guidance. We are constantly sold the lie that our dream life is hard to create and out of our control. When you take time off to simply rest, you realize you have more control than you think. We are expected to keep busy, power through, and push ourselves to pursue our dream life. If you are feeling disconnected from what your soul is calling you to do, feel unclear about your life's purpose, or that you are not living the life or doing the work you are meant to do, you are not alone. Many of us feel the calling but lack clarity because we are not making time and space to strengthen this connection. Our society simply does not encourage us to, so we must decide that our dreams are a priority.

Our life is filled with endless to-do lists that focus on what everyone else needs from us. These lists rarely involve taking time to commit to your soul connection. This must end today if you truly want to bring your dreams to life. It is time for you to make the space and time to answer your soul calling and take action on your dream.

This can feel hard because the connection to your soul is meant to be a challenge. To get started, you will need to agree with yourself to connect to your soul every single day. I invite you to begin with the journaling prompts I provided. As we move through the 21 days, I will give you more insights to strengthen this connection.

If you are new to spiritual and personal growth, it is best to start with simple tools. There are five key areas I have found helpful when you feel disconnected: (1) your soul calling, (2) your inner authority, (3) your superpower, (4) your story, and (5) your path in life. These five areas work together to help you connect to your true calling and tap into your potential.

The easiest way to strengthen this connection is by finding the best mindfulness tools that work for you. To help you do this, you will first need to understand your Soulchetype, or your Soulfulpreneur Archetype, which we will dive into on day 6.

Plan a Soul Date

Exercise

Do you know what your soul is calling you to do?

I've had a lot of conversations with people who tell me connecting to their soul feels extremely difficult. They feel disconnected and have no idea what their soul is calling them to do. So many things can get in the way of us strengthening this connection. Often, we fear stepping into our soul calling because of what others will think of us, Hello Karma. Start by being patient with yourself. Set the intention before you go to bed that you want to strengthen your soul connection.

Journal daily.

And have fun!

Do things you enjoy.

Spend time with people who you love and who lift you UP. Make the decision to make this process easy. Remember, your soul calling can be challenging, but you can always strengthen this connection.

What is your soul calling you toward? I invite you to plan a soul date this week. Think of something you've wanted to do or a place you've been thinking about going. Go to that place this week. Do that activity this week.

Day 2 Journal Prompts

Start where you are.

Questions to ask yourself:

What do I think about daily?

What have I been able to bring into my life and work efficiently?

What has been challenging to bring into my life that I truly desire?

When I sit still with myself, what do I hear?

What is the answer when I ask for guidance on the next steps?

What action can I take today without putting anything in the way?

Remember that I have everything I need within.

The answer is not outside me.

It lies in the skills and knowledge I already have.

Day 3

Trust Your Inner Guidance

What are you hesitating from taking action on based on external reasons?

I first decided I wanted to work from home in Hawaii when I was sixteen years old. The internet entrepreneur wasn't really a thing back then. I couldn't even imagine what work I could do from home. I just had a dream.

For the next few years, I would take daily aligned action. Take the following steps. Allow people with good intentions to support and guide me. I kept going even when it looked like it wouldn't happen. Release any doubt. I distanced myself from anyone who tried to doubt my dreams and sour my thoughts. I kept going until I reached the destination.

For so long, I had been running away from my soul calling. Feeling like I was not good enough to answer the call. Feeling like I was not "ready." Feeling like I did not know enough to answer it. To step into my calling fully.

But this was all a lie. A lie to keep me from going bigger. A lie from stepping into who I was being called to be out of fear. Because I felt scared. I didn't want others to see me in a way that seemed too out there or disconnected from reality.

The truth was, I knew what my calling was all along. It was, and is, to help bridge the gap between the spiritual and the practical. To help guide those of you who are new to tapping into your own gifts, feel more seen and heard as you navigate the uncertainty of your path.

You see, you are not behind in life or in work. You are exactly where you are meant to be. And even if the road feels windy, dusty, and uncertain right now, there is nothing wrong with you. There is nothing wrong with feeling like you have no idea what to do with your life right now. I am here to normalize feeling off-path. I am here to tell you that if you feel lost, this is an invitation to go within, to stop looking externally for the answers, and to be with yourself.

I know this can feel scary and not the answer you sought. But this is why I am here. To guide you, so you don't feel so alone as you take this next step. The answers you are looking for are not on Instagram. They are not in your inbox. They are not even in this book. They are within you.

I am writing this book as an intuitive guide to help connect you back to yourself. To look at the dreams, you put on the back burner. To answer your soul calling. To connect to your superpower. And to stop feeling wrong about where you are in life. Because where you are is beautiful.

No matter what idea you failed to take action on, where you ended up, or whether or not you feel accomplished, it was all by design. And you can start to design the life you truly desire by taking daily aligned action.

It starts by acknowledging that it is not meant to be easy every day. Some days you will feel in the flow, and others will feel like you are pushing a boulder uphill. In the world of instant gratification and seeming overnight success, we think challenges are not typical. But they are. Life and work are meant to be challenging. But at the same time, it is not meant to be unbearable. You are meant to experience joy, love, and happiness. Your work should not be grueling. Even if some days are hard, every day should not be difficult.

Once you connect to your soul calling and accept it as your purpose instead of pushing it away, more things will start to unfold in a way that feels fresh and free. Once you acknowledge that your gift is yours and yours alone to express, you will feel like you are on top of the world. Once you accept your destiny and acknowledge the path ahead, you will start to move forward.

During the next 21 days, I invite you to take this journey with me. To dive within and be open to inspired guidance. To listen to your inner voice. To stop looking externally for the answers. And to start moving toward your dreams.

Day 3 Journal Prompts

The story you are telling yourself about your dream.

Questions to ask yourself:

What stories am I telling myself that are serving my dreams?

What stories am I telling myself that are blocking my dreams?

What stories am I telling myself that are keeping my dreams from manifesting quickly?

What new story can I tell myself today?

In what way am I pushing my dream away?

In what way am I bringing my dream closer to me?

What story are you telling yourself about this dream?

How can you enhance this story today? Make it more inspiring? Uplifting or concrete?

Day 4

Tap into Your Superpower

What are your greatest gifts and talents?

In 2017, when I struggled to connect to my greatest gifts, my mentor gave me a book called The Strengths Finder. According to this book, we all have a set of strengths, and often they are so innate we have no idea what they are. The book is filled with many strengths, many of which I had never heard of before, with their definitions. At the back of the book is a unique code to take a test on the StrengthsFinder website. The test asks you a series of questions that take about 20 minutes. The goal is to answer each question quickly within a few seconds. You are not meant to ponder the answer; it is all about using your intuition and selecting the solution based on your first instinct.

At the end of the test, it provides you with your top-five strengths. I am sharing this with you because my top strengths were based on words that I would have never used to describe myself; however, each one deeply resonated with me. I had been struggling with one of my strengths in particular because I started to consider it a weakness. This strength is ideation.

While you might not think that having tons of ideas is a weakness, it can be overwhelming as an entrepreneur. I felt like I was being pulled in so many different directions because of my thoughts. Once I realized ideation was my greatest strength, I began to see it as my superpower. This allowed me to channel my creativity in a way that motivated me instead of holding me back. If you have not taken the Strengths Finder test and are struggling with your gifts, I highly recommend it. You might find that what you see as your weakness is your biggest strength as I did.

My superpower is_____.

Over the last several years, I have found this to be the hardest question for people to answer. We tend to be oblivious to our gifts even when others point them out to us.

My superpower is ideation. I used to think it was a weakness and something that held me back from picking my one thing in life. But then I realized that all my ideas were my one thing. I am a creative spirit who is here to help others align their purpose and passion. I would not be here without all the ideas that led me to the place where I belong.

If you are struggling to answer this question, rethink it. Your superpower could be disguised as what you believe to be a weakness.

I cannot recommend the StrengthsFinder test enough, especially if you feel disconnected from your gifts, talents, and skills. It also helped me choose the tagline for my coaching and digital course business, Bridging the gap between Work & Woo.

Did you know woo is a strength? Woo stands for winning others over. If this is your strength, you should choose a job where you interact with many people throughout the day. Although it was not one of my top strengths, when I came across it in the book it inspired me to infuse it more into my work.

Woo is an important strength to have in business because you cannot do it alone. It would help if you had others to help it grow, no matter your industry.

Another powerful way to uncover your Superpower is by understanding your numerology chart. In 2020 as I was deepening my spiritual understanding, I was drawn to angel numbers and numerology. I decided to get certified as a numerologist and use it as a tool in my coaching business.

We focus on five different areas when looking at your numerology chart: soul, karma, destiny, gift (superpower), and path number. Each area is a strength or a challenge. These key areas are based on your birthday, also known as your Soul Blueprint. Your gift number, which I love to refer to as your superpower, is the last two numbers of your birth year. For example, if you were born in 1982, you would add $8 + 2 = 10$. The number ten would be your gift number.

Each number has its own energy and characteristic. When the number is in your gift position on your numerology chart, it is naturally a strength. How cool is that? If you want to find out what your strength is based on your birthday, I have created a quick numerology guide for your reference. Once we learn about your Soulfulpreneur Archetype, you can use this information to help you unlock more of your potential in life and work.

To learn more about your numerology chart, enroll in the Decoding your Birthday workshop: nadiabernardy.com/birthday

Decode your Superpower

Quick Numerology 101 Guide

1. The Artist, soul-led and highly creative
2. The Negative Mind, able to set clear boundaries
3. The Positive Mind, open-minded and charismatic
4. Heart-Centered, humanitarian who loves giving back
5. The Speaker, can elevate others with their voice
6. The Master Manifestor, can easily create their dreams
7. Confidence, strong-minded and independent
8. Unlimited Energy, abundance of effort and action
9. Ability to master skills over the long term
10. Bold and magnetic just by being yourself
11. Strong connection to the spiritual and practical

Day 4 Journal Prompts

Look for common themes.

Questions to ask yourself:

What common themes do I see around the dreams I have been able to bring into my life easier?

What common themes do I see around things I have found challenging to manifest?

What stories am I telling myself about my desires, and how can I start to rewrite them?

How does my dream make me feel?

How can I strengthen my conviction about my dream today?

What areas do I need to focus on to take the next step toward my dream?

Look for common themes.

Day 5

Discover Your Path

Feeling behind in life and work?

I have always believed the road to success looked different for everyone, and because my mother was always there for me, I set a clear vision of how I wanted my life to look when I was 16. Due to my mother's health, she was unable to work, and although her health was deteriorating, I was always so grateful that she was there for me when I got home from school. Living in Maui, many parents struggled to stay afloat, which meant working multiple jobs and, as a result, were never home. But my mother was always there, and I saw the value of that and decided I wanted the same when I had kids.

I had no idea what I wanted to do with my life, but I knew it had to be something where I could work online from home. I wanted to have a career and be successful while always being there for my family. I never doubted this was possible, and my mother had a massive part in that. She taught me that the power of your mind was all you needed to create the life you desired for yourself. So, I made a very clear vision for my life, never doubted that it would manifest, and took the next steps that would lead me to my dreams.

I genuinely believe there are always crucial people who show up in your life with a purpose to help you along your journey. And because my mother was so sick, I intuitively knew I needed to connect with people around me who could support me on my path. Although I was in high school, I did not feel that graduating was the right path for me. In my attempt to avoid my mother's failing health, I would often ditch school to go on adventures around Maui with my friends. It was not because I was not smart or did not believe in school. It was just that I felt like I needed to find another way. I ended up dropping out of school, getting my GED, and attending community college in what would have been my senior year of high school.

It was during this time that everything started to make sense. I felt like I was doing what I was meant to do. At community college, I met a school counselor who changed my life forever and put me on the path I had been searching for. When I told him that I wanted to do something creative in which I could use my skills to also work online one day, his first words were, "Well, have you heard of graphic design?"

Of course, I hadn't and immediately wanted to learn more. I started taking art classes, photography classes, and anything that resembled graphic design because it was not taught anywhere on the island. When I applied to art school and got in, I was elated. But everything fell apart when I realized I could not just go off to college and leave my sick mother.

I was devastated, put my dreams on the back burner, and got a job at a restaurant. Everything felt hopeless until my mother's brother reached out because he had not heard from us in a long time. When he talked to my mother and could hear how sick she was, he offered to help. This led to my mother moving to Indianapolis, which allowed me to move to New Mexico to live with my grandmother so that I could go to art school. Looking back on this time, it was one of the most complex decisions of my life as it was the first time I would be living apart from my mother. I learned that sometimes your path will feel difficult, but everything you experience is meant to support you even when it is painful.

If your path feels challenging, be open to receiving help and guidance from those around you. Some people truly love you and want to guide you along your path.

I want to remind you that feeling off path in life and work is normal. Even though society would have us believe that we need to have everything figured out all the time. There is nothing wrong with you if you feel unclear. I have been studying different spiritual modalities since starting my awakening. I became fascinated by how much insight numerology gave my clients around their soul calling, superpower, but the most prominent breakthroughs came from understanding their path.

If you listen to my podcast, I share the realizations I began to have utilizing numerology in my work. Path numbers are a numerology concept that I find the most comforting. While your gift number, or superpower as I call it, is a strength in your chart, your path number is unique. The path number in particular is traditionally seen as a challenge; however, I view it as a strength and a challenge depending on your life circumstances.

Sometimes in life and work, you feel like you are going in the right direction. The sun is shining, the weather is sweet, and as soon as this beautiful day starts, it begins to rain. The road starts to curve, and before you know it, you are lost.

While society would have us believe that being off-path in life is unacceptable, I am here to remind you it is 100 percent normal to be off-path. You are not meant to have it all figured out all the time. It is called having the human experience.

It may not feel like it, but the path you are currently on will lead you to everything you desire. It can appear that others have taken the straight path to success, happiness, and fulfillment, but everyone's journey is filled with twists and turns. Even if it looks perfect online. Stay positive, keep going, and you will find your way.

Day 5 Journal Prompts

Create an affirmation for your dream.

Journal an affirmation specific to your dream.

Focus on words that will help bring your dream toward you.

Don't worry if your words are still rough ideas.

You can finalize your affirmation as you gain more clarity on your dream.

Do I feel behind or off path when it comes to taking action on my dream?

If I feel behind, off-path, what steps can I take today to strengthen this area of my life?

What stories am I telling myself that are serving my dream?

What stories am I telling myself that are blocking my dream?

What am I telling myself that is keeping my dream from manifesting quickly?

What new stories can I tell myself today?

Day 6

Soulfulpreneur Archetypes

Uncover your Spiritual Entrepreneur Archetype.

I want to help uncover your Soulfulpreneur Archetype to guide you further on manifesting your dream. We all have a calling that we choose to embody in this life; however, many of us are working against our purpose instead of with it. No judgment, as I am guilty of this as well. Anytime you feel resistance, like you are forcing yourself to do something or just do not want to do it, this is a sign you are working against your true calling and not with it.

Working with our calling makes us feel energized and like we are on the right path. If you do not know what your calling is, don't worry. I am here to guide you to connecting back to yourself. If you used the numerology guide in the superpower section, you already know what your greatest gift is. It has been there all along, and now we are going to dive into what your soul is calling you to do by learning about the seven Soufulpreneur Archetypes. I discovered these archetypes reading numerology charts for clients. Over two years, I started to uncover a very distinct pattern.

There were seven main archetypes that kept resurfacing in people who felt called to take action on a big dream. I will be going through each one, and I want you to tap into which one connects back to you. Although most of us have one main archetype, you may find yourself drawn to more than one archetype. I have a little secret for you—most people connect to at least three. There is this societal pressure to be one thing and to excel at one thing only, and while that might be easy for some, most of us struggle to identify as one thing. This is because we are multi-passionate, multidimensional beings, and it is okay to experience different areas and qualities.

For example, you might resonate as a healer, which might even be your superpower. But you are also an artist. By understanding these two archetypes, you can then use them to work with each other instead of against or force yourself to pick one path if that does not feel aligned.

Once you understand each archetype, pay close attention to which one speaks to you the most. Which one resonates? Where have you infused these archetypes into your life and work, both currently or in the past? Have you envisioned yourself using any of these archetypes but are holding yourself back? Be honest with yourself. The archetypes were designed to help guide you to back to yourself and your true calling.

We are all born with intuition, and we can tap into it at any time. Your soul already knows what you are here to do—you just need to listen.

Soulfulpreneur Archetypes

The Soulful Teacher

The teacher is downplayed dramatically in our society, which often baffles me. We all have a thirst for knowledge; as a teacher, you are here to quench that thirst. It is a noble and respectful archetype to embody and one I am stepping into daily. You are meant to help those who have questions find answers. To elevate this awareness from where it is to where it needs to be, so people can live strong and meaningful lives. To be educated is to be elevated.

Your purpose as a teacher is to learn what you are most passionate about, what fills your soul, and then educate others. As a teacher, there are endless possibilities for the direction you can go, and picking a subject that brightens you up is ideal. Do not hold on to the idea that teachers are not well compensated. To have knowledge is to be wealthy, and you can earn as much as you desire. You are not limited to what society or the patriarchy deems as a teacher's salary. You charge in alignment with what you have to give.

Teachers are honored, looked up to, admired, and essential. They can choose to teach any age in any subject in whichever manner is best for them. This is actual power and should always be celebrated. If you have a passion that you cannot stop talking about and fills your heart with joy, if you have always wanted to share this knowledge and find yourself teaching even without realizing it, then this archetype is your soul calling. It is your natural talent, and you can move into this gift by first acknowledging and utilizing it whenever you have the opportunity.

Gather some friends and hold an online workshop on a topic you love. Find others who want to learn about a subject they are curious about but know nothing about and educate them. You can work for an institution, create your own school, or work for yourself. In this age, your knowledge is in demand.

Let go of any ideas that say teachers are not robust and abundant. Think of teachers on the same level as doctors and lawyers. Without knowledge, you are destined to fail. Without the right teacher, you are lost in life. We have all learned from teachers, and yet there is a disconnect. You can be a part of the connection that brings teachers back up to where they should always be—on top.

Do you resonate with being a teacher? Have you pushed down this archetype because of stigma? Are you currently a teacher and feel like you are not being treated fairly? It is time for you to use your gift and step into it fully.

The Elevated Healer

The healer is a beautiful soul who is here to energize the planet. You may think of a healer as a naturopath, a massage therapist, or an energy healer. But the healer can also use this gift in other areas, such as creativity, through words, and other work areas.

The healer can tap into source energy and infuse it into every area of their life and work. If you feel like you can never run out of energy, you are a healer, as most of us only dream of having your vibrance for life. It is important to note that while some of these gifts are in more alignment than others, we all can step into all these archetypes if we so choose.

They just need to be developed, like riding a bicycle or learning how to surf. One of the best ways to align with the healer archetype is through breathwork. The Elevated Healer has a solid connection to the abundance of nature. Working with your breath can bring more of this abundance into your life and work. Even if this archetype is not your specific calling, breathwork is still beneficial for anyone curious and wanting to learn more. I would encourage you to always work with a professional.

The Abundant Artist

The abundant artist is the magical creator who can take visions and dreams and turn them into anything they desire. Embodying the artist is such a beautiful calling, yet like the teacher we tend to push it down. Society tells us all these crazy beliefs, and we become programmed to believe them.

The thriving artist is the message I am here to share with you. The abundant, prosperous artist who is fully supported by their gifts at all times. The sky is the limit as to what you can create. Tap into the true artist, and allow your expression to fly. My mother was a true artist, and so was my husband. They were both created in entirely different ways, and the people who were meant to enjoy their work always found them.

Release any outside opinions about what an artist can and cannot be. Connect with the artist within, and start creating what your heart is begging you to share. There is often so much resistance as an artist to move with our gift and not against it.

Do you find yourself daydreaming? Do you draw, write, or paint just because? Do you feel bursts of inspiration? Do you daydream about colors? Do you fantasize about unseen worlds? Then you are an artist. Start where you are and do not pressure yourself to move forward. Flow into this space, and let your gift naturally unfold how it is meant to.

The Thriving Creative

The thriving creative might seem similar to an artist, but there is a crucial difference. While both celebrate the unseen, a creative has a very strong ability to take an idea and bring it to life in a more tangible way, while the artist creates to create. I know this because I started my life as a creative, studying graphic and web design. I used my ideas to create branding, logos, and beautiful designs, and then I would move on to the next.

While an artist might stay working on a piece for months or even years, a creative will move on to the next idea more seamlessly. The creative has tons of ideas they want to share with the world. Sometimes this is for others, and sometimes it is for themselves. A visionary will keep taking aligned action until the project is created, while the artist will create until the art feels finished if that makes sense.

If you are creative, you might find yourself drawn to content creation, the act of creating multiple pieces, digital art, or photography. While all these creations are a form of art, most of the time, these are projects with a specific purpose instead of creating just to create. They are tangible and serve a particular purpose. It is essential to note the difference to see which type most closely resonates with you.

Not sure where to start? Creativity is your guiding light, whatever that looks like for you, whether it's writing, drawing, singing, painting, or even mixed media. Start with expressing yourself in a natural way, and pay attention to what inspires you during the process. Finding the best creative outlet for you may take time, so don't rush the process. Creativity is KEY.

You are meant to share your gifts with the world if you are called to create. I always tell my clients that creation leads to clarity.

The Inspired Intuitive

The intuitive is someone who can tap into their inner knowing easily. We all have this gift, but some of us specifically have it in our soul blueprint, so it comes more naturally. But we can all strengthen this gift, and I would encourage you to do so through some of the meditations in this book. This will also help you to gain more insight and clarity into what you are meant to do and which archetype resonates with you.

If you are someone who feels like you know things or can sense things, you are intuitive. If you could use intuitive as a profession, there are lots of ways. I use it in coaching sessions to help people connect back to themselves. I am using it to write this book. I use it to do numerology charts.

My entire business is built on my intuitive gifts. You can also use your intuitive gifts to earn a beautiful living if you so choose. You just need to believe it is possible for you and start to strengthen this gift. Grounding meditation is a beautiful way to start. So are visualization techniques shared in this book.

The Divine Leader

Most of us can quickly state whether we are a leader or not. Most people who are leaders already know they are leaders and the ones who don't will have a sense of longing. They will feel like something is missing. They know they are not stepping into their power but don't know why.

If you are a leader, you are taking charge, but not in a pushy way—in a way that is here to guide and support others. You are not a dictator but someone who can help others become who they are called to be. You have a great sense of self and can communicate in a way that people understand and inspire them to move with you and take aligned action. You have a great sense of the direction you are heading. You do not second-guess yourself and can make decisions quickly and easily.

This means you have stepped into your power as a leader, and if you feel the exact opposite but have the desire to be a leader, do not discount it as not being your archetype. It just means you have not fully tapped into this calling. But the good news is that you 100 percent can, and this book is intended to guide you to use your archetype to manifest your dreams. So if you want to be a leader but aren't one yet, it is available to you, and you can be the leader you desire—imagine you can be—not the stereotypical view of a leader but the leader that resonates with you.

Work on communication. Be aware of where you are struggling to make a clear decision. Organize your thoughts and your space. Look at areas of life you excel at, and look for opportunities to guide others in a way that is natural to you and your style.

The leader also focuses on mastering skills over the long term, for example, learning to surf over three to five years and then leading others on a surf retreat. I also want to note that leaders lean towards the divine masculine or the divine feminine in their life and work. The divine masculine leaders are bold action takers who are inspiring just by being themselves. While divine feminine leaders tend to lead with grace, are refined in their approach to guiding others, and present themselves to the world in a way that makes them feel good internally, not by external factors.

The divine leader can embody both feminine and masculine approaches to life. However, they tend to lean towards one more than the other. If you feel called to be a leader, journal on ways you can inspire others.

The Spiritual Leader

The spiritual leader is the leader who bridges the gap between the physical and metaphysical realms. You are here to help people connect back to their souls. This is a significant purpose to fill, and most spiritual leaders start off on a different path in life—typically the creative, unless they feel truly lost. Like the leader, you will communicate and use your natural abilities to guide others. But this guidance especially relates to spirituality and helping people tap into their gifts and connect to the spirit. If you haven't guessed yet, I am a creative who transitioned into a spiritual leader and am walking this path now. It often takes spiritual leaders going off the path and feeling entirely out of alignment before realizing this calling; however, you will always come back to this place and help those ready to hear this message. The fact that you are reading this book is not by accident, and you are prepared to step into your true gift no matter what it is.

Suppose you often find yourself pulled between the practical and the spiritual, feel a higher calling but lack clarity, and have the desire to dive into spiritual studies. In that case, it is no surprise that this archetype could be speaking to you too.

Now that you have learned about the different archetypes, it is time to journal one that spoke to you. You might already know, still feel lost, or feel a connection to two or three or more. Wherever you are, that is okay. This is a journey, and you will come to the place you need to be when you are ready. Do not get discouraged. Keep going. Do the clearing meditation daily, and journal out your ideas.

The Divine Dreamer

I specifically left the divine dreamer out of the seven archetypes. I believe we all possess the ability to be a divine dreamer, some of us more than others. It most aligns with the abundant artist archetype and even the thriving creative, but I did not want to place any stereotypes on what a dreamer is because your way of dreaming is unique to you. I see the dreamer as more of a trait, state of mind, and way of being than a calling or an archetype. I also feel that we should all allow ourselves to dream without feeling pressured to be "labeled" as a dreamer.

This is why I refer to you as a soulfulpreneur on the podcast. Because I am encouraging you to take action. While I feel that dreaming is more associated with the daydreamer who lives in their mind and never takes action, I believe that dreaming is necessary no matter your archetype, and so I will leave it to you to determine what dreaming means and looks like to you.

The one thing that always bothered me when it came to spirituality and manifesting, in particular, was this general understanding that to manifest, you just sit around all day, meditate, and things will just appear. While I believe in miracles and would encourage you to believe the same if it supports you, this is not how it works. Yes, our beliefs are important. Yes, giving time and space to ourselves for prayer and connection to the divine is key, but you must take physical and mental action.

It does not need to be complicated. It can be aligned. Hard work is only required if you believe it is necessary to get the job done. I'm not saying you do not need to put in any effort. But I am saying the action can be seamless if you believe it is. We often receive back what we put into the universe.

Soulfulpreneur Archetypes

Day 6 Journal Prompts

Which Archetypes resonate with me and why?

Am I drawn to other Archetypes, and why do they speak to me?

What is my soul calling me to do right now, and how does that relate to my archetype?

Do I really feel connected to my gifts and talents?

What is my superpower and how can I use it to take action on my dream?

Do I feel closer to my path in life and work now that I know my archetype and superpower?

What am I being called to create today based on my archetype and superpower?

Find Your Woo, Find Your Why

When you are in true alignment with your passion, your purpose will be clear.

Day 7

Soul Story

The power of your soul-led story

Using your story to help others is a powerful way for you to start to gain clarity on what dream you are meant to live. We are often so focused on the fact that we feel lost, stuck, or unclear that we forget how our story can help others. I would invite you to think back about how far you've come and the things you have accomplished thus far. Your dream lies within your story.

There is a saying: "Don't look back; you aren't going that way." That saying has never personally resonated with me. Because while yes, it is essential to live in the present, there is so much to learn from our past experiences. The key is not to dwell there but to use what you have learned to give back to yourself and others. What lessons have you learned that can help others? I have included some journaling prompts to help you think about this fact.

Use your story to serve (help others) people who need what you have to give. They can learn and grow from you and your experiences, and you can help someone avoid or get through mistakes, and challenging times and help you release and forgive yourself for things that did not go the way you planned.

Not only can your story be helpful to others, but it can also allow you to move forward and grow. We are all carrying things from our past that are holding us back. We try to avoid them and pretend they are not there. But it always comes to the surface when we least expect it. Forgiving yourself for mistakes you've made, and situations you wish would have happened differently, allows more space for you to grow and live a more peaceful life. I realized during my spiritual awakening that I was holding on to so many stories from my childhood that were keeping me stuck.

Looking back, I realized that I was not even fully clear about my situation. Much of it had to do with my perception as a child, which means I was not in the mindset yet to fully comprehend the situation. I was viewing it from a child's eyes and not an adult's. Once I looked into these experiences further, I realized that I had utterly misunderstood this issue. Many of these things I was holding on to in fact, had nothing to do with me but were complex relationships between adults. For example, I lived with my mother and paternal grandmother when I was very little. My mother and grandmother had two completely different ideas about how they wanted to raise me. My mother was a bohemian artist with a strict Catholic upbringing. My grandmother was also Catholic, but she was very proper and formal.

Once I could see my role in the experiences I had as a child, I understood that they were out of my control. This allowed me to release this weight and focus on what I could control. It is compelling to look at your past and let go of the things that are holding you back from taking action on your dreams.

Soul Story

Exercise

Connecting to your super soul story will provide the insights you need to start taking action on your dreams. Who you are meant to help and how you are meant to help them is in the experiences you have already had. Use the Soul Story Framework below to clarify the transformation you are meant to experience. It will also be powerful for you to share this transformation with others who are meant to learn from you. This Soul Story Exercise was inspired by The Hero's Journey by Joseph Campbell.

Feel free to choose your own colors, but here is a legend of what each statement represents. Highlight each message with the corresponding color to understand how you will use each part of your Soul Story.

Soul Story Framework

SOUL SEARCHING AND KEY PAIN POINTS (green)

SOUL CALLING (orange)

REQUIRED SHIFT AND TRANSFORMATION (red)

RESOURCES AND CURRICULUM EXAMPLES (purple)

EXPERTISE YOU CAN TEACH (pink)

CORE DESIRED FEELINGS (blue)

SOUL SEARCHING STATE:

I was at my lowest/most frustrated/most challenged/most stuck point when I was _____.

I was craving _____, _____, and _____.

In order to achieve _____,

I had to shift from _____ to _____.

To learn more about this, I turned to _____, _____, _____.

When I achieved/made it/shifted to _____, I felt _____, _____, and _____.

I went from _____ to _____ so that I could _____.

Day 7 Journal Prompts

Soul-led Story Journal Prompts

What is a problem you've solved? An obstacle you've overcome? A skill you've mastered?

What is the most painful thing you've ever been through? There is power in pain.

What is the most inspiring thing you've ever done? There is also power in growth.

What makes you different than anyone else on the planet?

What is the #1 thing people ask you for help with?

Ideation Is Your Greatest Gift, Not Your Weakness. We all have different gifts to share with the world. Never compare yourself to the person standing next to you, across from you, or in the same niche as you. Always be true to yourself, and your talents will shine.

Day 8

Inspired Ideas

Ideation is your greatest gift, not your weakness

With a background in creative arts and marketing, I started playing around and dreaming up different business ideas. My first job out of college was working for a wholesale company helping them to rebrand their e-commerce platforms.

I started thinking about different businesses I could start in the e-commerce space. I would come up with an idea, the branding, and the name, start the process, and then fall out of love with the idea. This happened so much my husband started to tell me to just pick one thing and focus on it. But I couldn't. Nothing felt right. At first, it was just the creative dreaming stage, so there wasn't any pressure. I was working through my ideas.

One idea I had was to sell beach cruiser bicycles. Living in Hawaii, I thought it would be a super fun thing to sell online. I found a distributor, and created a website, and when I actually figured out the math it didn't make much sense. I gave up on the idea and never officially launched it.

This happened with several other ideas until I finally stopped going down the e-commerce path. I still have tons of ideas for e-commerce shops. If you need one, just let me know.

I believe this was the graphic designer in me. In school, we were taught to create branding for clients—logos, taglines, fonts, and websites. But then you walk away. It is then up to the clients to put in the work, invest money in inventory, and sell. I was just there to create; my brand was to be a designer.

I have had ideas for days and still do. For a long time, it drove me absolutely crazy because I would come up with an idea, fall head over hill in love with it, and before you knew it, I was bored and ready to move to the next one.

I still have a few ideas I am holding on to, still attached to the idea that I will one day create the vision and make it a reality.

In being crystal clear, you might be telling me, "But what if I have tons of dreams? What if I have so many ideas that I cannot pick just one?"

If this is you, I would 100 percent agree with you, as I am also a multi-passionate, multitalented creative. This is something to celebrate, as most people can't even come up with one idea, let alone one hundred. Having too many ideas is a gift. I have learned to appreciate.

The cure to shiny-object syndrome, as many like to call it, is to focus on the one dream you can take action on now without putting anything in the way. You must also focus on the ideas that are truly coming from your soul and not from the external.

There are a lot of wonderful ideas, and you may have a few because you saw something, which is quite possible, given the fact that we are connected to more information than ever before. But I would invite you to ask yourself, "Is this idea truly something I want to create? Or is this idea based on what others expect of me?"

When we are crystal clear, we allow our ideas to flow. They will take shape in a way that feels easy and fun, leading me to my next point, resistance. I'm sure you have felt wanting to take action, but something always seems to get in the way. You can't quite get yourself motivated, and everything seems to be going wrong.

Remember that you do not need to take action alone. I will guide you as you move through the next twenty-one days. I will not lie; some days will be harder than others. But in order to manifest our dreams, we must move through the resistance to get to the other side.

This doesn't mean we force anything to create. This means we give ourselves grace, time, and space while creating. We are often so hard on ourselves and our own worst critics. I would invite you to be kind to yourself through this process.

Inspired Ideas Prompts

Ideation is your greatest strength, not your weakness.

Steps to help connect to your inspired ideas:

- Set intention before bed.
- Have a journal ready and with you at all times.
- Write down any and all inspiration that comes to you.
- Using a pencil is critical.
- Use voice memos to record your thoughts.
- Ask for this connection to be strong.
- Ask for guidance and support during this process.
- Allow words, thoughts, and ideas to flow.
- Do not hold yourself back.
- Do not allow outside forces to distract you.
- Create a sacred time to do this work.
- Be open to inspiration at any time.
- Be open to receiving inspiration all around you.

Inspired Ideas Light You UP

Day 9

Aligned Action

Work and woo modes

When I started coaching in 2018, it was in direct response to a dream job—I had loved for so long that I no longer felt in alignment. As I worked to uncover what I was meant to do, it came to me that I was running away from what was right in front of me.

I had always had a strong belief that the work you did was in direct reflection of what you loved, what you were good at. I did not subscribe to the idea of earning money from a job just to earn money, apart, of course, from college, when I worked random jobs, like most of us, while I studied what I actually wanted to do—graphic design and commercial art.

So, when I found myself at this place, I realized I had disconnected myself from my belief, and all I had to do was go back to that. It seemed so simple, and yet I was making it so complicated for myself. If you feel it is so hard to figure it out right now, it really is right in front of you—you need to recognize it. Once I realized that my biggest passion was doing work I loved, I decided to create an entire company around it and help others connect with what works and winning over others (woo) looked like for them.

Once I did that, my day job started to turn into a dream job again. I began to earn promotions, bonuses, grants, and incredible opportunities to help me on my journey. The company even paid for me to live and work in San Francisco for three months teaching and public speaking, which helped me tap even further into my gifts.

Your purpose is staring you right in the face, but you may tell yourself that you can't do that for a living. Well, I hope I am living proof as I sit here on my sofa, on Maui, writing this book and working from home for myself, coaching female entrepreneurs, and creating online courses that anything you want is entirely possible. I quite literally made my own work—work that I love, work that lights me up. This is not a fantasy; this is your reality. You need to believe it. I know what you're thinking: Well, that's easy for you to say. You grew up in Hawaii. Your parents must be rich.

I had a very unique perspective when it came to wealth. I grew up with a single mother who could not work due to her health. I also had a grandmother whose second marriage was to a millionaire. I went to private schools my whole life while living off government assistance. I wore name-brand clothes while also shopping at goodwill. I had the influence of a wealthy lifestyle even though we were far from wealthy. It gave me a non-traditional view of what was possible when attracting my desires.

So how did I create the life of my dreams? It is easier than you think. I told myself it was possible, did not obsess if it would happen, and started taking the aligned action I will share with you.

But first, you need to acknowledge what works and woo mode you are in. What is work and woo mode? It is the mode that allows you to ebb and flow between taking action and allowing things to come to you quickly and naturally without resisting it. In fact, there are five main modes, and we will understand them all so that you can start working from a place of ease, working with your gifts and not against them. But before we can get to the work and woo mode, we need to understand the work mode.

Work Mode

Work mode is where 99 percent of the world operates. It is the place of putting everything in the way before you can get to the thing you truly want. You want $100. Well, it can't just appear, or can it? Now, before you think I've gone totally woo-woo, hear me out. Have you ever experienced desiring something, and a friend shows up with it? Or do you really want some ice cream and find some in the fridge but need to remember buying it?

We have all had these experiences in which things seem to naturally unfold; however, they tend to be few and far between. For the most part, things take considerable effort and are uphill battles. But I am here to guide you and show you a different way, a seamless manner. But before we can get there, you need to start where you are, which I will assume is in work mode. If you've already advanced from there, keep reading because it is important to be clear on work mode so that you don't get sucked back in.

In work mode, earning money requires hard work. Projects require a lot of effort to finish instead of allowing things to flow naturally as they should. If you are currently in a job that is out of alignment for you, then you are in work mode. Society would have you believe that the most important thing has work that supports you financially. But the most important thing is doing work that elevates your spirit, not drains your soul.

This is why 85 percent of people are unhappy at work because they were taught that putting their soul desire on the back burner was required. But you must connect back to your soul calling to live a fulfilled life. Working a job that drains you is not the way your soul intended you to live. The quicker you realize this, the faster you can shift toward work that feeds you. This book is designed to help you make this shift by understanding the work and woo modes so that you can focus on that one dream you have been pushing down for far too long. It wants to come to light and be shared with the world.

Work and Woo Modes

Ah, work and woo mode is where I love to help clients get to because it starts to lift the heavy load. You are still taking action and putting efforts into your desire, but at the same time, allowing for the space for things to happen naturally. You are not forcing the outcome; you are typing things out, experimenting, using your natural gifts, and using your inspired ideas to shape things. It is a creative process that allows you to work with the resistance in a way that enables you to move forward and take action.

Things still might be challenging at times, but that's okay. Where there is a challenge, there is an opportunity to find another way. A way that feels easier. A way that feels aligned. Please pay attention to the work you are doing now, and take stock of the areas you are making more difficult than needed. In what way can you make them easier on yourself? Even if you are in your day job. Remember: I tapped back into my work and woo mode when I was out of alignment with my dream job. And the result: I manifested a new easier role, earned more money, and celebrated my achievements within the company.

You can make a job you despise easier if you genuinely believe in the work and woo mode. Stop fixating on the things about your current job you dislike, and start focusing on what you want it to be like and what tasks you enjoy, and watch how things shift. This is the same for your business and any area of your life. You need to be open to receiving another way—a way that will work best for you and your gifts and talents.

Before long, you might not even remember the old way of doing things because your work has provided you with more and better opportunities, or maybe you have manifested another job opportunity. If you have ever worked on a project in which things felt like they were unfolding the way they were meant to, then you were in work and woo mode.

This mode allows you to take action, and put in the effort, and then allow the work to be easy. It is a balance of using your conscious mind and subconscious mind in a way that serves your endeavor seamlessly. This is the place I hope to guide you toward in this book. Manifesting is not about sitting around and daydreaming all day. It is about allowing your dream to unfold by taking action that is right in front of you. The aligned action will always be available to you. It is always action you are open to take.

Woo Modes

When you start to ebb and flow between work and woo mode, woo mode is when the real magic starts to happen. This is where I often find myself as things just start to unfold beautifully without me feeling like I had to put in any effort, such as manifesting the perfect client or finding an opportunity to share my gifts.

A perfect example of woo mode is when you think of ice cream, and your friend shows up out of nowhere with your favorite flavor because they were just thinking of you. Something similar has happened to you, and it can start to happen a lot more if you live in a state of woo mode. You just expect for amazing things to happen, you truly believe something will unfold in your favor, and so they do.

This book is a perfect example of flowing in and out of work and woo mode for me. As I write this sentence, it is Christmastime, but I already know it will elevate my work, business, and ability to help people because I believe it, feel it, and desire to make it an impact and to serve.

This book will make waves and help so many people. I can feel it and trust the process as I write the words, even though it has yet to unfold. If you live in a state of woo mode and believe that things are always working in your favor, things will be seamless for you, even if things get off track or you find yourself back in work mode now that you know what woo mode feels like. Trust the process to guide you back.

When you look at the desire you manifest in twenty-one days, be open to it unfolding in a way that requires as little resistance as possible.

Woo mode is when you set the intention for a dream or a project, and out of nowhere, help appears. A friend calls to tell you that they have the perfect thing you need. You get an email from someone you have never met inviting you to do a collaboration with them. You discover new software that will make completing the project easier and faster than ever imagined.

These are just examples of what woo mode could look like. Woo mode is when you are crystal clear on what you want, and things seem to show up to help support you and guide you to getting that work done. Some would call this divine timing, God, angels, the universe, the source—whatever resonates with you, a higher power is supporting us on this journey. But it is essential to know and understand that this higher power is not outside us but within us. You have the ability to tap into woo mode at any time. You need to believe that it is available to you.

We have been conditioned to think we need to look outside ourselves for the answers. My goal is to help guide you back to yourself, your inner guidance, and wisdom. It is waiting for you to tap into it at any moment. I find that using the work and woo modes to help me see how powerful I truly am through making my impossible dreams a reality is the most concrete way to align with my superpowers.

Advanced Modes

There are two modes that I have personally yet to master, but they are worth mentioning to help you to even further gain what is possible. This book is meant to guide you through the first three modes, as most of us are living in work mode, but more modes are available.

These two advanced modes are woo-woo mode and spiritual home.

I'm sure some of you have also experienced woo-woo mode. I know I've had experiences that I cannot explain when things happen or appear without me doing anything. This may appear as unexpected money. You open your cabinet, and there is a book you need to remember buying but need. You may even receive a prize for a contest you don't remember entering. The truth is things always happen without us truly understanding them. Some call these miracles; others say it is divine intervention.

Whatever these occurrences are, it is vital that you remain open to this support and never doubt it. It is very challenging to understand how things can happen without us doing anything, which is where the resistance to these occurrences lies. But if we remain open to allowing these interventions, our lives will be much easier. Accepting miracles is easier said than done, but at least remain open to the possibilities as they occur every day.

The spiritual home is your divine connection to one and your actual connection to the source. We are all tapped into the source, but this is on an entirely different level, and one my soul does not desire because I like the contrast of having the human experience. It is why our souls come here, but some people want to connect back to the source, and it is important to note that nothing is impossible.

Since this book is meant to help you align your mind, gifts and spirit to manifest your desires and live your dreams, we will focus on the first three modes in this book.

Taking Daily Aligned Action

Aligned action is intentional, and it is aligned with the gifts and knowledge that you already have. If the dream you are picking is something you can't take action on right now, in this moment, it is out of alignment. This is not to say that you cannot create this dream. You have a responsibility to get yourself into a place where the action is aligned for you by bridging the gap.

So what do you need to do to make this step toward this dream something you can take right now? And please do not say money. Because while money is an essential resource in the world, it is not why you cannot make your dreams a reality. You are the only thing getting in the way, so let's not put the energy of money as a barrier to entry because it is not.

Let me give you an example. I have always wanted to start an online boutique. My first job out of college was working for a wholesale company designing e-commerce websites. I was so excited because I graduated from college in 2008 with a job in my field, which happened to be during a recession. And when I say that no one graduated with a job in their field right away, that is not an understatement.

When I started school, I set the intention to graduate with a job. Instead, the last semester in college, while everyone was focusing on finals, I was focusing on finals, working part-time in the accounting office of a hotel, and applying for anything and everything that had to do with web and graphic design. I was applying for jobs I was way overqualified for, jobs I was way underqualified for, and everything in between.

There is this stigma in design school that you will graduate with a job at a copy shop, like Kinkos or FedEx, and have wasted time getting a private art school education. But I did not care. I applied for those jobs, too, because I did not want to graduate, not doing something somehow related to my field, even if it wasn't at a fancy-pants design firm.

I remember seeing an ad for a part-time junior graphic designer. The pay was way less than I wanted, and the hours were minimal. I knew I was overqualified. This would have been the perfect job for me while I was in school, not upon graduation. But I swallowed my pride and applied anyway. Not only did I apply, but I treated the interview like it was for a top-notch design firm with all the benefits. I dressed up very professionally. I had my portfolio ready, and I walked into the interview confident that I was applying for a full-time dream job with benefits.

The interview was with the owner of the company. She was from Texas and reminded me of Brené Brown. She looked at my portfolio and she said, "You know you are way overqualified for this position."

In my mind, I thought, I know I am way overqualified. But I replied, "It is important for me to start a career in my field, even at an entry-level." One project grabbed her attention as she flipped through my portfolio, which was all mock design clients I had done at school. I had done a paint bucket watercolor design for a pretend T-shirt company.

"Oh, I absolutely love this design! Tell me about this piece?"

As I explained to her, I left out that it was not an actual client and talked about it as if it were something I had done for a client who loved the design as much as she did. She was fascinated as I explained it to her, and I could see her falling in love with the idea of me working for her wholesale company.

"Well, I just love this, and it speaks to my ideas and some of the designs I want to create here."

"I'm going to have to think about this."

I felt terrific and also unsure all at the same time. I knew I was overqualified, and she knew I was overqualified, but now what does this mean? I felt like she was going to hire me, but the job wasn't necessarily a dream. I went back to working on finals, preparing for graduation, and interviewing at various places.

Finally, a week before graduation, Jeannie called me. "I have decided to create a position for you. After looking at your portfolio, I realized we need you here. How would you like to be our in-house web and graphic designer? With your own office?"

I could hardly believe it—my office with a job doing exactly what I went to school to study. I was floored! My dream job had been created out of thin air. I started the week after graduation, and it was a time in my life when everything felt right and like I was on the right path.

I worked for the company for almost two and a half years and was eventually promoted to internet marketing manager, another position created for me. I got to travel all around the country, going to trade shows, and it elevated my skills far beyond what I had learned in school. It prepared me for in-depth knowledge of the e-commerce industry, online marketing, and sales.

To this day, I'm forever grateful for that opportunity.

After about two years, I felt the pull to do something different. I had an idea for my own e-commerce business, but I never ended up launching it because another dream job was waiting around the corner.

Day 9 Journal Prompts

How do I work best?

Am I truly tapping into my gifts and talents for my work?

Do I tend to work alone, or am I open to receiving help, support, and guidance?

How can I make my work and life easier, simpler, and more enjoyable today?

The Aligned Action Will Always Be Action You Can Take.

Always

If you are not taking the Aligned action, it is because you are making it harder than it needs to be.

- The action needed to manifest your desire will ALWAYS be Action you are able to take.
- Action is journaling.
- Action is meditating.
- Action is having fun.
- Action is effort.
- Action is creating.
- Action is work.
- Action is whatever it needs to be for you to move forward.
- But it does not need to be complex.
- It does not need to be hard.
- It can be as simple as you desire it to be.
- It can be the next step right in front of you.
- It can start right now.
- Today
- What Aligned Action will you take to move closer to your dream?

Day 10

Creative Windows of Time

Do you tell yourself you do not have enough time?

The first meditation I ever recorded was the perfect day guided meditation. It was a project I applied for when I was working in tech. So I decided to record and enhance it to make it available to those struggling to create their ideal week.

The idea behind the creative week is to first focus on your perfect day, or as I like to call it, your dreamy day. Start by writing out how you want your day to look without scheduling meetings or making time to run errands. The idea is to allow your day to flow exactly how you imagine it to.

Then you look at your day and create the next day and the next day until you have an entire week. Once you are finished, you look at your real-life schedule and adjust your day in any way you can to represent your dreamy day, even if it is something small. Before you know it, your ideal week will start to unfold the way you have planned it.

One of the things I wanted for my ideal week was not to have any meetings on Mondays. I wanted it to be a day of creativity where I could write and share my thoughts. It took some time, but I stopped scheduling meetings on Mondays. I don't book any appointments with the doctor or run errands. Instead, I started recording podcast episodes every Sunday. I meet with clients and students on Tuesdays, Wednesdays, and Thursdays. Friday is errand day, and appointments are reserved for Thursdays as a backup option. Saturday is family and friend day, and Sunday is family and podcast day.

Create your ideal day, then allow that to create your ideal week. Before you know it, you will be working the way you envisioned. Do things come up that sometimes throw me off? Of course. But overall, when I look at my week, it is close to my ideal week. Instead of dreaming and guessing and wishing that you had the schedule you wanted, make small changes every day to get closer to this ideal week. This exercise does work.

Ask yourself how do I work best? For example, am I a morning or night person?

But before we start, I want to share some key insights that will help smooth the process.

The first is creative windows of time. Please stop saying that you do not have time. From now on, start to say you have more than enough time. It does not matter if you work 80 hours a week, have young kids, and have a demanding social life. The moment you start saying you have time, times start to open up for you.

I remember when I first started rebranding my service-based business into a business and mindset coaching and course business. My daughter was three years old, and it felt like we had 800 birthday parties to go to every weekend. I thought, "She is only three." How is her social life more packed than mine?

Instead of telling myself I did not have time to work on my business and take my daughter to her social events, I made them work together. Whenever I left the house, whether for a birthday party, a playdate, or just running to the grocery store, I brought my work. I'm not saying to celebrate hustle culture and burn yourself out. Be open to opportunities to receive inspired ideas for your dreams everywhere.

I remember one time my daughter fell asleep as we were leaving a birthday party. So instead of driving straight home, I took the opportunity to pull over at a park. I took photos of the gorgeous view of up-country Maui and journaled out a blog post idea. My daughter never knew the difference, and because I was open to this creative window of time, I could tap into some inspiration.

The more I focus on creative windows of time, the more they open up to me. This exercise I would invite you to do is "your ideal week and perfect day." I have included a perfect day-guided meditation at the back of this book and as a free download. I created my ideal week and perfect day while working a schedule that was not ideal. Even better if you are not currently working and living the hours you want to live. Use this exercise to help you create the schedule you wish, and do not be surprised when your ideal week and perfect day become your reality.

The goal of the exercise is to first start with your perfect day. Then, without putting anything in the way, write out exactly how you want your day to go. Get very specific. What time do you want to wake up, not what time should you wake up? For your perfect day, what time would you wake up?

What would you do first? Would you go outside for a walk? Would you get a cup of coffee? Would you meditate? Get ready for the day? Whatever this looks like for you, write out every detail. Write out what you would eat for breakfast. Who would you want to spend your morning and day with? Would you rather be alone? Would you work from home or not work at all? The sky is the limit for your perfect day, so do not hold anything back.

Now focus on your ideal week from Sunday to Saturday. How does this relate to your perfect day? Is every morning the same? Are some days workdays and other days for self-care? Or would you be in vacation mode? Again, the sky is the limit. Do not hold back.

I invite you to journal on this for twenty minutes or so and do not leave out any details. This exercise is incredibly powerful, and I can speak from experience, as I am currently living and working my ideal week and perfect schedule. So don't be surprised when you are living your ideal week and perfect day too.

The next step is to focus on your intention. What is your purpose for the life and work you wish to create? What inspires you about this life? How will your work encourage others? Whether you realize it or not, when you act on your dreams, you will inspire others to do the same.

Be sure that your intention is clear. For example, my intention with this book is to help you take action toward your forgotten dream. I want you to leave this book feeling more connected to yourself and inspired by the future. Because my intention is clear, I can write from a place of clarity and focus.

The Perfect Dreamy Day

Exercise

Create your ideal schedule.

We often go through life's motions without even stopping to think about what our dreamiest day would look like. What if you could start to imagine this day so clearly that it becomes your reality?

I invite you to do this exercise before starting your twenty-one-day journaling practice.

This exercise is not meant to limit you in any way. Instead, it is an invitation to dream bigger. Bigger than you could have ever imagined. To release any idea that you cannot live your ideal day. You have to conform or constrict your day because of your current schedule. Because of your business, your work, your school, your spouse's schedule, your family's schedule, or even for your children, if you have them.

Before you say, "But I'm not selfish," I invite you to reframe your words to, "But first, dream bigger."

Before everyone else's agenda pops into your day, what do you want? What does your ideal, perfect dreamy day look like?

But more importantly, what does this dream day feel like?

What do you desire to do as soon as you wake up? Not what are you expected to or think you must do, but what do you genuinely want to do upon waking up?

An even more powerful exercise is to set this intention before you go to bed. To set the purpose for this dreamy day in your dreams. Your dreams are powerful. Your subconscious is free and open. Tell your dreams what you desire for your day.

Do not hold back. Let the pen flow, and write out this perfect morning.

Once your morning is finished with all the perfect details just for you, start with your afternoon.

Listen to Perfect Day Guided Meditation audio at nadiabernardy.com/perfectday.

Before you say someone else has already created it or you don't have the time, I want you to imagine that this dream is your reality. Visualize yourself already having this dream now.

How do you feel? Is there a sense of ease? Are you remembering all the little details of this dream? Do you feel inspiration coming through?

This is the feeling I am here to connect you to so that you can start taking action over 21 days. But before we start, I want to share with you some key insights that will help make the process smoother.

The first is creative windows of time. Please stop saying that you do not have time. From now on, start to say you have more than enough time. It does not matter if you work eighty hours a week, has young kids, and have a demanding social life. The moment you start saying you have time, times start to open up for you.

You are still catching up in life and work. Even if you are not where you desire to be, that does not mean you still can't get to where you want to go.

It sounds simple, yet we often use the power of our minds in ways that do not serve us—in ways that work against our dreams. We allow outside influences to take us off track and doubts about setting in.

Before we know it, years have passed, and we have yet to take a single step in the right direction. Our dreams get tucked away inside our minds. We look around one day and realize we still needed to manifest exactly what we want.

I am here to remind you that you can still pick up that dream and start to act. This book is meant to be a guide to help get you out of your comfort zone and to reconnect you with something that is still tapping you on the shoulder. That one nagging thought or long-held dream.

If you don't know what your soul is calling you to do, you are where you are meant to be. A big part of the work I am meant to do in the world is to help you connect to your soul calling. Once you do that, you can start taking the aligned action and dream bigger.

Are you ready to dive in?

Day 11

Flow Is the New Hustle

How to stop celebrating hustle culture

I know hustle is a buzz, especially in the United States, but I have never subscribed to this concept. Maybe because I grew up in Hawaii and had been working online from home for the last eleven years while looking at the coconut trees. But your work should come naturally and at the right pace for you. If you constantly feel burnt out and stressed, that is a sign you are not in alignment. Get back into flow by taking things one step at a time. There is no need to rush the process, as things naturally unfold how they are always meant to.

Many of us find ourselves in hustle culture unintentionally. We want to have a balanced life with ease a flow. Work a great schedule, have the weekends off and take time to travel. But the reality of what that looks like is typically far different than we imagine.

With deadlines, the pressure to get promoted, the pressure to keep up with society's expectations, and the pressure we put on ourselves, we find that the balanced life we thought we were creating is a far cry from the reality we are living.

Even though I was working online from home before it was a thing, I found myself sucked into hustle culture. In a matter of months, my dream job turned into a source of great stress. My team was turned into what we called the dumping ground, and the random projects were assigned to us left and right. From dealing with high-profile press cases with Airbnb hosts to luxury Airbnb listings having an urgent need.

I stopped to wonder how I had gotten here. But then I realized that my work was not out of my control. Even though in the moment, it felt like I had to do work I didn't enjoy, I really had a choice. So I sat down and thought about how I wanted my ideal work to look. What did I want to do? How did I want my days to unfold?

It made me realize that I had always believed that the work you do should be something you enjoy. The work you do should be based on your gifts and talents. So the whole reason I was working online from home was to enjoy my life and work.

Within a week of having this realization, Airbnb announced the Recharge and Refresh Program that I mentioned earlier. The even more remarkable fact is that not only did I get paid time off to rest, but my team got a significant upheaval when I got back. My supervisor ended up leaving the company at the time, and not too long after I got back from recharge, a new supervisor was assigned.

The new supervisor was the complete opposite of the last one, and she immediately became an advocate for helping my career. The opportunities started to come in left and right. From being told there was no money in the budget to travel to all of a sudden being invited to meetups in Portland, Oregon. Bonuses were given when we were told there would be no bonus. I received more raises and stock than I had ever been given. I even received a grant to help me with my coaching certification.

While it might feel like your life and work are out of your control, it is up to you to determine what you will tolerate. For example, once I realized that I am not available to do work I do not enjoy, things shifted quickly for me. Within a matter of months, the job I was dreading became my dream job again.

I don't know exactly how this will unfold for you, but things will change if you get to the core feelings you want to experience. For example, if you are unhappy with your work, write down what you want your day to be like. Do not focus on what you don't wish to; focus on what you want. The way this unfolds for you could be through a new role opening up within the company, a friend might reach out about a new job with their company, or you might see an ad for a great unique business opportunity.

However, these opportunities can only come if you focus on your current situation. If you are overworked, stressed out, and in an endless cycle of not enough, you will continue to experience this. But if you focus your energy on living a peaceful, balanced life doing work you love, things will begin to change.

Use the creative windows of time exercise and continue to take daily aligned action.

What matters is that you truly believe that life is not out of your control; you are in control. I understand it does not always feel that way; sometimes we want to run away and cry. But know that even if things are not the way you desire them to be, this is just an opportunity for you to design them the way you want them to be.

That is why I wrote this book. To help guide you toward that first desire, that dream that is 100 percent attainable in twenty-one days so that you can see your power and understand what is possible.

Right now, how would you say you make decisions? Are you quick to say no? Or do you constantly find yourself saying yes almost to a fault? I tend to be more of a people pleaser—saying yes to things I do not truly want to do and then paying for it later. However, I have learned over time to say no. Especially as a business owner, I have to be very intentional with my time. It is not that I do not want to help people or be there for important moments. But if you say yes to anything and everything, your creative windows of time fill quickly.

Remember when I told you about all the birthday parties my daughter would get invited to? Well, it got to the point that while I was finding creative times to work and keep my daughter's social calendar packed, I needed to start saying no.

I had to be very intentional with my time, and spending four hours at a birthday on a Saturday was exhausting and very time-consuming. It was not that I did not want to celebrate my friends' kids' special events, but it was starting to impact my energy levels.

To keep growing my business, raise a family, and have time for self-care, I started saying no. For an entire year, I rarely went to a birthday party and slowly started adding more events to the calendar as my schedule opened up. It was a period that served my life and works well.

We need to give ourselves permission to say no. We need to look closely at where we spend our time and only do things helping us get closer to our dreams. This doesn't mean you do not have a social life, but you will find that you will go through a period of your journey where you have to choose: Do I want to work on making my dream a reality today? Or do I want to hang out at the beach all day?

I live in Maui, so I get drawn to the beach, and sometimes we do need a break. But when you look at where you spend your time overall, you can clearly see where and when to make adjustments.

On the flip side of saying yes to everything, we can also say no way too much. Some of us say no to a fault. We miss out on great opportunities and are so rigid with our time that we miss out. Pay attention to where you are saying no, and think about what would happen if you said yes. What would happen if you did nothing?

This is what I like to call making decisions from your positive, negative, and neutral minds. Once I learned this, my life and work changed entirely. I now look at every single decision I make from these three perspectives. What would happen if I said yes? What would happen if I said no? What would happen if I did nothing?

The next time you come across a decision and are quick to say yes or no, take a moment and ask yourself these questions. You might be surprised by the opportunity you have been blocking yourself from by saying no too often and draining yourself unnecessarily by saying yes without thinking.

Day 11 Journal Prompts

Create boundaries in my Life and Work.

Pay attention to what you are quick to say yes and no to. Unfortunately, we often agree to things we do not actually want to do and it can get in the way of us taking action on our dreams.

Try to make every decision through a yes, no, and neutral filter by asking yourself, "What if I say no? What if I say yes? What if I stay neutral and do not respond?"

How will saying yes to this opportunity help me achieve my dreams?

Where am I saying no and possibly blocking myself from opportunities?

If I stay neutral or do not give an answer right away, how does this make me feel?

Reference your perfect dreamy week and the creative windows of time section if you struggle with this area in your life and work.

Day 12

Create Your Dream Rituals

Night ritual, journaling, and meditation

Have you ever suffered from burnout? It's that feeling that you have given more than you can provide and are met with exhaustion like you could not go on another day living and working the way you are. If you haven't experienced that, I am telling you to rest before it occurs because I would not wish burnout on anyone. But if you have, then this will probably sound all too familiar.

In 2017, I suffered from burnout. I had been working in tech for almost seven years with a baby in tow and a small business—I was done. I needed a break. But at the time, like most of us, I was celebrating the hustle mentality. Don't get me wrong; hustling works. I hustled for years and got everything I wanted. Finally, I was living my dream life in Hawaii with my beautiful family, working online from home, and building two side hostels. I was living the dream, but at what cost?

I was creatively stifled, exhausted, and disconnected from my soul. That sounds like it could be more dreamy. So when my therapist told me to take time off, I almost asked her to repeat those words in English. Take time off to rest? Do people do that? Is that a thing? I cringe now, thinking how disconnected I was from self-care. Now you hear self-care thrown around like nothing, but you might have been speaking Japanese at the time.

Fast forward to today, and self-care is part of my weekly, dare I say daily, life. There is no separation between work and play. It is all integrated in how I do life now. I take breaks when I need to and drink water, which sounds easy but is also super easy to forget. I make sure I am giving back to myself consistently. Because if you do not realize it yet, giving back to yourself, taking time off, resting, and treating yourself is not selfish; it is required to live a whole, vibrant life. It is necessary so that you can give back to others as well as yourself.

The years I spent waking up barely having a cup of coffee and working on my laptop for hours on end without taking a break is the furthest from healthy that I can imagine. And because my results were my dream life, I kept going until I hit a wall. Then, figuratively, I was forced to take a break. If that had not happened, I assure you I would still be forgetting to drink water. Universe, help us all.

If this is you, I urge you to take a break. Take time off. Do not worry about your finances. I do not care how practical you are. Set the intention to leave your financials to the universe. It will work out, and your mental well-being is way more important than a paycheck. I know we all have bills, and I am not telling you to quit your job, but you need to create space and time for yourself. If you still need to do that, return to the Perfect Day exercise and prioritize yourself ASAP.

Rituals are important. Are you a morning person? No? Me neither. This whole wake up at 5 a.m. routine is just another way to drill in the hustle mentality. Don't get me wrong; if you are naturally a morning person, then that's wonderful. Wake up at sunrise. I do it a few times a year, and it is beautiful.

But I am not naturally a morning person. I am naturally a wake-up, chill-out, and get to-work once-I am awake person. And so I have given myself permission to work during the times that most align with me, not the other way around. I know what you might say: "Well, great for you. I still have a 9-to-5 job." I get that. I had a 9-to-5 job, and they are great if they are serving you and serving your dreams. But if they are not, it is time to start making adjustments.

You are the creator of your own reality. Unless you love it, this job is not the creator of your time, finances, and freedom. You have just permitted your job to be this force in your life. Even if it is impossible to see right now, you can take this power back.

It starts by you recognizing that you are in control of your life. You are creating your experience, and you can make the dream life and work you feel called to. But you have to connect back to your soul calling, get on the path, and tap into your SUPERPOWERS. That is what this twenty-one-day journey is all about. Are you ready?

Great! First, I invite you to start with your rituals, particularly your nighttime ritual. I know everyone and their grandmother talks about a morning ritual, but trust me, if your night is jacked up, your morning will be too.

So let's start with the night. What are your current habits once the sunset sets? How are they currently serving you? How are they fucking you up? Let's start there so we can create a new ritual. I share with you a few key things that have helped me and my family have a better nighttime ritual.

Once the sunset sets, I adjust our lighting. Lamps go on, ceiling lights are turned off, and I light candles, and set the tone.

Ebb and flow between feeling clear and unclear between feeling on path and off path. It is a dance that we need to find grace, joy, and love in because it is about moving through and with unsettled feelings.

Those who talk about having a great morning routine are not wrong. Setting yourself up in the morning is vital, but you cannot have a good morning with a shitty night routine. It all starts with the night, and once you can get yourself in the right state of mind before you go to bed, the morning is yours for the taking.

I found that lighting is critical to transitioning from the business of the day to the night. As soon as the sunset sets, I turn on the dim lamps, plug in the fairy lights, light a candle, and set the tone for winding down.

As a woman, I also focus on self-care, and I recommend you do the same, regardless of whether you are a woman or a man. Self-care is so key for us taking action on our dreams because before we can give to our ideas, we have to offer to ourselves.

I have become obsessed with holistic beauty and spend forty-five minutes to an hour doing the ancient technique of gua sha. It helps to remove stress from the day and relaxes my face like nothing else I have ever tried. I am also a massive fan of strong mint tea; sometimes, I use three bags.

Lastly, just like in the morning, I love to journal before bed. Writing helps me release anything from the day that did not serve me, and it helps me to highlight the things that I did. If you don't already have a nighttime routine in place, please create one for this exercise.

Don't worry about it being perfect. Some nights are not as peaceful as others, but the goal is to try to get yourself in a state of calm and release so you are not bringing anything that sucked into your next day. The last thing I like to do, especially if I am feeling uncertain, blocked, or stagnant, is ask for guidance in my dreams.

We underestimate our connection to a higher power while we rest. Sleeping is the perfect time to seek answers to things you have been struggling with. You can journal on these questions and then pray before you fall asleep. Make sure you have a journal by your bed in the morning, and be ready to write down the things that come to you immediately.

If I get a download or hit of inspiration upon rising and I don't write it down or use a voice memo immediately, I lose it. Don't let that happen to you; always keep a pen and paper handy.

I do not want to get into a lecture, but because I mentioned the voice memo, I want to talk about our phones. They run our lives. If you immediately say no to that, note how much you check your phone in a day. Check the hours. Don't get me wrong; the phone is an incredible invention, and I am genuinely grateful for it, but we are on it more than we should be. I am guilty of this as well.

For a long time, I blamed it on running an online business, so I "have" to be on my phone all the time. But the truth is automation is a miracle that all online business owners should use daily, so there is no excuse. Yes, I love getting on Instagram stories and checking in with my audience, but that only takes a few minutes.

Please create a ritual that encourages you to separate from your phone at night and first thing in the morning. You will notice the urge to pick it up right away, and the best thing I have found to fight that is to replace the notion with something else. For me, this is journaling and going outside to meditate. I stopped leaving my phone on my bedroom nightstand and purposely kept it charging in my office.

Find a place you do not need to go to first thing in the morning and plug your phone in. If you go to the kitchen first thing, charge your phone in the living room. If you go to your office first thing, set it in the kitchen. Put it in a place you do not naturally gravitate to in the morning.

Create a sacred space for you to spend your mornings. For me, this is on my lanai, also known as a deck. If it is raining heavily, which it tends to do where I live, then I have a corner of my living room I use. This place should be set up just for you and have nothing to do with work. Add some things you enjoy, something cozy, and make this space your morning ritual.

Even if you feel like you do not have time in the morning because you are off to the races with work and family responsibilities, it is still vital for you to create this space. The space will start to open up for you if you make this space nonnegotiable for you in the morning. You will find the time, and your creative windows of time will start to open up.

Similarly, having a place you go to away from your home is helpful to get inspiration and connect back to yourself. For me, it is a forest on up-country Maui. I love to roam around aimlessly and daydream about what I want to create next. For you, this might be a park, a bookstore, or a lookout spot. Wherever this place is, make sure you go there at least once during your 21-day Dream Bigger exercise.

Why Journaling Works

Why have some mindfulness tools stopped working for you

After I suffered from burnout in 2017, I realized I had gotten away from a practice that gave me immense peace: journaling. I started journaling profusely when I was in high school. It was a way to get my thoughts out and feel more connected to my feelings. My mother was getting sicker at the time, and none of my friends could relate to what I was going through.

Journaling was my escape, my sanctuary, my sacred space to be myself. I would fill pages and pages of my journal. Everywhere I went, my journal went too. One day when I left my journal in my friend's car by mistake, and she read it with another friend. She questioned me on what I had written, including my thoughts about her. I was mortified. My private thoughts revealed. Looking back, I realize how careless I was with my journal.

It didn't have a lock on it, I didn't make it clear that no one could read it, and I left it out for anyone to see. But, still, I guess I believed there was this unspoken understanding that your journal, like your diary, was private and personal.

After that, I still journaled but wasn't as honest as I once was. I found myself holding back my words and writing from a place of generalization. Once I moved to New Mexico for college, journaling fell by the wayside.

I had forgotten how much I loved journaling until I took time off from work during my three-month recharge from Airbnb. During this time, I picked up this ritual again and have not looked back since. I constantly journal, day and night. Anytime I have an idea, I write it down.

It helps me stay centered and focused on what I need to take action on and what I need to wait on. I have included journal prompts throughout this book to help you move through the 21 days.

I've been told by several people that they struggle to journal. You might be one of them, so I included journal prompts to help you with this powerful process.

The key to journaling is not to have any judgments on your thoughts. Write as if you are going to need someone to read your words. Don't hold yourself back from letting your true ideas flow onto the paper. Even if you feel stuck, write that you feel stuck. Add that to the page even if you don't know what to write.

Once you make this practice a daily habit, your words will flow. Use the journal prompts I provided to help you, and be bold and use a journal prompt for multiple days. If you find one of the prompts helps you get your ideas out, use it again.

Keep a journal by your bed, on your desk, or wherever you feel the most inspired, and write when you feel called to. I find it best to write in the morning, but you may do so after lunch. Do what works for you, and only force yourself to journal at any specific time if that would be helpful for you.

I refer to my main journal as my anything-and-everything journal. This journal is my special place to write anything that comes to mind without resistance, judgment, or limitations. I've also found it helpful to have a journal for my business to journal ideas I want to take action on. If this is helpful for you, then I would try this as well. Keep a journal for your general thoughts and one for the things you want to take action on.

If you find this practice challenging over time, try recording your voice and refer back to the journal prompts in this book.

The Art of Gratitude

Practice being grateful for the little and big things

Need help? Find time for yourself today. I understand that not everyone can take a week or even a day off to give back to themselves. But try to find time within your day for self-care. Don't let the business of society dictate how you treat yourself.

Look for an hour or, at the very least 30 minutes where you can focus on yourself. Of course, don't mindlessly watch TV or listen to a podcast (trust me, I love a good podcast too), but this is about being with yourself.

Take a moment to highlight your strengths and the things you are grateful for. Then, focus on lifting yourself up, and don't make it about anyone else.

One thing that has genuinely helped me with feeling more connected is practicing the Art of Gratitude daily. It has increased not only my mindset but also my awareness of how important self-care truly is. So start with feeling grateful and see how things begin to shift.

If you are still struggling in this area, I have created a FREE Art of Gratitude e-journal to help you bring this truly beneficial practice into your life. nadiabernardy.com/gratitude

Beautiful Self-Talk

Pay attention to the words you speak daily

The words you speak, write, and think daily are powerful.

With that power, you can change your life, rewriting the words that are not serving your desires. Pay attention to the words you use daily. Affirmations and journaling are great places to start.

But I want you to know you can even go deeper by accessing your soul calling. This is deep work. Transformational work. But it's genuinely beneficial if you are not experiencing the desired outcome.

The soul is where the majority of our daily actions and habits live. By shifting the outdated actions that are not moving you forward, you will start seeing the results you truly want. Start where you are right now by creating affirmations, and even try recording your voice. Be open to sharing and teaching what you already know to people who need to hear what you say. Even if you do not consider yourself an "expert," your wisdom is valuable and can help others.

Be open to connecting with a straightforward thing you can share each day. It does not have to be profound—although it can be—but if you are new to this, focus on something simple, helpful, and valuable that has benefited you in your life.

Be mindful of the way you speak to yourself. Remember to use kind words, encouraging words, and try not to be too hard on yourself. Create affirmations for yourself, and even try recording your own voice. This is the best way for you to train your mind to think in a way that benefits your wants and desires.

As you know, Sundays for me are for self-care. There is a sacred place called 'Īao Valley State Park, one of my favorite places on Maui. The energy there is so powerful.

It left me feeling recharged and refreshed, which is so important before starting a busy work week. It reminded me to tune in to my own self-talk. I created a beautiful self-talk-guided e-journal with powerful "I am" affirmations. Download your free e-journal at nadiabernardy.com/selftalk

These inspire you to bring positive affirmations into your daily habits. The way we treat ourselves is so fundamental.

Start by keeping your affirmations very simple. Soon you will start to catch yourself anytime you say something negative to yourself. You can then easily flip it to a positive "I am" statement.

Day 12 Journal Prompts

What areas do I need to focus on to take the next step?

What steps can I take today to get closer to my dream?

What am I putting in the way? Am I taking the path of least resistance?

What words can I use to bring this dream closer to me?

How do I feel about this dream today?

Be the Visionary You Wish to See in the World.

Day 13

Visionary Board

Vision board meets mirror work exercise

Have you ever heard of mirror work? A mentor introduced this practice to me, which has been life-changing. The idea behind mirror work is that you are speaking to yourself in a way that allows you to reframe the thoughts not serving you and your life. We tend to have words going on daily that are keeping us stuck. These words are on autopilot, and they never change until we stop to truly pay attention to them. Mirror work is the practice of speaking to yourself in a positive way, while also paying attention to the limiting self-talk. Once you become aware of the self-talk that is inhibiting you, it is easier to reframe it.

Start by standing in front of the mirror, look yourself directly in the eyes, and then tell yourself out loud how proud you are of your accomplishments, how grateful you are for your talents and skills, and how much you love yourself. If you have never done this work before, you may have words that try to downplay the praise you are giving yourself. This is common and simply an invitation to observe and then reframe.

If it feels extremely uncomfortable to do mirror work, you are doing it correctly. It will be awkward initially, but the intention is to do this practice daily. The longer you practice mirror work, the more impactful it will be on your life.

Mirror work impacted me and my work so much that I wanted to take it a step further. I have always loved creating a vision board and thought it would be powerful to combine it with mirror work. We often post little notes and mantras on our mirrors, but what if we turned the mirror into a vision board or, as I like to call it, a visionary board.

In high school, I had this beautiful circle mirror surrounded by shells. I got it from a garage sale I went to with a friend and her mom. I thought it was the most gorgeous mirror, and I honestly forgot all about it until I came up with the idea for the visionary board. I don't know what happened to it, but I must have given it away when I moved off to Maui for college.

I wanted to re-create this mirror as part of this process because it reminded me of a time when I was always dreaming big. Even in high school I knew I would move back to Maui one day and live near the ocean. Now that living a ten-minute drive away from the beach is my reality, I knew it would be decisive for me to bring a piece of that into my visionary board project.

First, I would invite you to think about this as a creative project to connect you back to things you love. I found a beautiful mirror with a blank wooden frame. Over the years of living in Maui, I have collected tons of broken shells, sea glass of all different colors, and some drift wood. I decided to create a shell collage around the mirror to represent the life I have created and help me bring in the dreams that have yet to manifest.

Think about something you have already made in your life and how you can use it as the frame for your mirror to create your own collage. This represents how powerful you are at manifesting and will help you feel confident in the dreams you are calling in now.

In everything that you create in your life and work, you are in the center of it. The house you live in, the car you drive, and the work you do is all being created by you. If you are unhappy with any area of your life, it is up to you to change it. If there is a dream you want to create, like the dream you are calling in now, it is up to you to first visualize it.

Creating a visionary board means being super intentional about what you are bringing into your life. I created a visionary board and included this book as something I wanted to manifest. I used it to see myself as a writer, a business owner, and a coach. I've used it to bring more money, travel, and fun experiences into my life and my family's life.

The visionary board can be used for whatever you want to call in. I like to focus on three specific categories, but you can also create your own. The first category is work, which relates to your career, business, or charity work. I write down how I want to feel about my work, the impact I desire to make, and how I want to help others.

The second category is a lifestyle, which includes where I live, travel, my family, and different experiences I want to have, such as learning a new exercise, like barre. The third category is money and wealth. This includes specific amounts I want to bring in, investments I want to make, donations, and ways to give back financially to my community.

Next come the images and photos of the items you want to call into your life. I printed most of my ideas based on photos I found online, but you could also go the old-school route and cut out images from magazines.

You may even have pictures of the items you want. If your dream does not exist yet, for instance, if you want to create a new product, find images that represent the purpose behind the creation. For example, if you want to create a new business, you can start by considering your branding colors, different names, or ideas for products or services.

Then write down mantras and affirmations in your own words. Our words are so powerful, and when we speak them out loud, it helps us anchor them into our minds. If you struggle to write your own affirmations, it is helpful to start with ones that resonate with you and then add your own spin.

I use a gold metallic sharpie to write down my mantras. Have fun with this part, and use your favorite color. The important part is that you write it down in your own handwriting. Refrain from printing out the words because you are going to be reading these mantras daily. The idea is to see yourself as the person who truly believes your words. It works better if you are telling yourself that your dreams are possible. It still feels unbelievable when you hear it from another person, but when you tell yourself, it is the truth.

Now comes the aligned action, which we will discuss on day 11. You should hang this mirror in your bedroom. When we first wake up, we are still sleepy, and our minds are much more susceptible to suggestions.

With you in the mirror's center, repeat the affirmations and mantras you have created while visualizing yourself already having the images you have pasted on the mirror. Do this practice daily until the images start to manifest. Once you have brought a desire into your life, replace it with a new one. The idea is that your visionary board evolves, changes, and grows as you do.

For you to start taking aligned action, you first need to see yourself as the center of your dream. Have fun with this project, and get creative.

Visionary Board

Exercise

- Find a mirror with a frame.
- Create a collage around the frame of items you love.
- Print out images of the items you want.
- Write out mantras or affirmations using your own words.
- Tape the images and mantras all over the inside of the frame.
- Hang the mirror in your bedroom.
- Every morning when you wake up, repeat the mantras.
- Visualize yourself already having the items in the images.
- Repeat this daily until the items have manifested.
- Once you manifest your image, replace it with a new one.

Day 14

Signs in Nature

Are you open to receiving signs?

We all have a connection to the divine, regardless of whether we realize it or not. This connection is always available to you, and you can build and strengthen this connection at any time. Like your soul connection, you are divine. The universe is you, and you are the universe.

I first started to strengthen this connection by receiving signs from the universe. These signs were mainly seen in nature. For example, when I sat on my lanai to meditate, a red cardinal would visit me, and it still does whenever I am thinking about something specific. I would also see the light faint rainbow in the distance and sometimes a bright full rainbow as a big bold sign.

I live in Hawaii, and while I knew these were signs, I needed more concrete evidence to help drive this point to others who are looking to strengthen this connection.

The key to connecting to these signs is to pay attention to your thoughts when you see them. The ideas are often fleeting, so this does take time to master. Over time, you will notice that when something has been on your mind a lot, the clarity will come to you in the form of a sign. The sign is not something you can force or dictate.

This is not about demanding you see a purple butterfly in the next five seconds. It is more about setting the intention that you are open to receiving a sign and trusting that the sign will be something you need to see.

For example, with the rainbows, I know that this means I am on the right path with my work. I started to notice that every time I questioned whether the work I was creating was what I should be doing I would see a rainbow.

It was similar to the red cardinal. When I would meditate, it was often to gain insight on whether I was taking the proper steps with my business. I would see the cardinal as confirmation that I was being supported on my path. It was not just about seeing the sign; it was what I was thinking at the time and the feeling I received. Every time I see a character, it gives me so much happiness. I know it is for me.

I invite you to also set the intention to receive a sign. Trust that whatever appears, whenever it appears, it will be a sign you can trust is for you. Start paying attention to your thoughts.

This can be tricky at first, and this is when I started to wonder if there were other ways to receive signs. Even though I trusted that the characters in nature were not a coincidence, I wanted more confirmation. If you are new to receiving signs, you probably want the same.

I wanted to know if there were other ways I could receive confirmation on the signs I was seeing. This is when I discovered numerology and, later angel numbers. Pretty quickly after I found angel numbers I started to notice 1111 daily, and as time went on, I began to notice other sequences of numbers, such as 121, 838, 555, 444, and 333. Every time I looked up the meaning of these numbers, it resonated with me, and I became increasingly enthralled with receiving signs.

Not too long after, I read my numerology chart and was shocked by the accuracy of the numbers. If you listened to my podcast, I share what my numerology chart says about me. But all the longing I had been experiencing in 2017 was my transition from path 2, the creative, to path 11, spiritual leader. My soul was calling me to teach, and I am, writing this book and sharing my message with you.

My goal is to help you take action on one dream you can accomplish in the next 21 days, so that you can see what is possible and continue using this method to create even bigger dreams. I've used this process to start a podcast, create online programs, and learn meditation. I then took this method to set a long-term plan to help me with the writing stages of this book: writing the rough draft, editing the rough draft, editing it again, finalizing the book and designing the cover.

Dreams are made on the other side of taking daily aligned action. For a long time, I believed—and I think many still do—that dreams just appear. Don't get me wrong; miracles are real. We see miracles every day, but in most cases, to make your dreams a reality requires you to first believe in them and then take action daily.

The action will always be one you can take, and this book is meant to guide you toward bridging the gap between where you are now and where you desire to go. You can use this guide for as many dreams as you want. But to start, I recommend starting simply with a dream you are truly aligned with. As the smaller goals start to take shape, move on to the bigger dreams. Each manifestation will prove that you have the power to create anything you desire in your mind.

I ask for guidance whenever I move through unfamiliar territory in my business and life. Every time I pause to ask a question for the last week, I look outside and see a red cardinal. I've also noticed the wind pick up every time I end my morning meditations. These are coincidences, but I do not believe in coincidences. Everything in life that happens is meant to be and is in response to you. Are you paying attention to the signs the universe is sending you?

If you want to learn more about numerology and angel numbers, I have created a special workshop called Decoding Your Birthday, Numerology 101. This will give you insights into what the numbers mean in your specific numerology chart and how to use them to clarify your true calling.

To learn more, visit nadiabernardy.com/birthday

Day 14 Journal Prompts

If your dream has manifested, focus on gratitude today.

If your dream has yet to manifest, sit in faith that it will unfold when it is meant to.

Ask yourself, "Am I open to receiving signs?"

What signs have you noticed this week?

What is your immediate thought when you see this sign?

How does this sign make you feel?

Keep taking inspired action.

Be kind to yourself.

Rest and recharge if you need to.

Create whenever you feel called to.

Dream Work

The art of connecting to guidance in the astral realms, and using this knowledge to clarify your life's purpose.

Have you ever had a dream so real you woke up with your heart pounding? What if I told you that the images you experience in your dreams are more real than you think.

I discovered dream work while writing this book after experiencing dreams that felt so real I could not deny their meaning.

After my mother passed away, she started to visit me in my dreams. From the first one I felt like I had just spent the day with her when I woke up. It did not feel like anything I could make up in my mind. The biggest reason for this was the way I felt during and after the dream. I undeniably felt that the experience was not made up but had actually occurred. The difference is the experience happened in the astral realms, deep in my subconscious, and not in the conscious mind, where most of us tend to think life is occurring from.

If you have never heard of dream work before, I like to refer to it as the art of connecting to guidance in the astral realms, and using this knowledge to gain clarity on your life's purpose.

One of the most powerful experiences I have ever had with a dream was during a workshop I took on dream work. I was meant to have this experience first before finishing this book so that I could share it with you.

Have you ever heard of dream recall? It is the practice of recalling a dream you've had before. I'm sure you can remember a plan that was so lovely you wanted to experience it again. Well, what if I told you it was possible to recall your favorite dream? Or even a dream where you desired more clarity. The dream felt so real you could remember the details.

While I've had several dreams of my late mother, I only had one dream of my late father; it was in 2012, not too long after I had moved back to Maui from New Mexico. I was walking with my father, who was this bright large angel-like figure. We were talking, and then it felt like all of a sudden, he needed to leave.

As he pulled away down this bright white tunnel, he kept repeating a phrase that I struggled to hear. I ran toward him as fast as possible, but the quicker I ran, the farther away down the tunnel he went. He kept repeating the phrase until I woke up in a panic. My heart was racing, I was terribly upset, and I could not remember what my father was trying to say to me for the life of me.

It had bothered me for years. But, after that day, I never dreamed of my father again.

When I took this workshop and learned that I could recall any dream I wanted, I immediately thought of this one. I thought, Now I can finally know what my father was trying to tell me, and maybe I can find out why I haven't dreamt about him again almost a decade later. As I was drawn into a deep meditative state, I found myself in a beautiful field with light green grass, beautiful mountains, a bubbly stream, and my father. What I was able to uncover wholly shocked me.

You see, for years, ever since having this dream, I always thought the entire dream took place in the white tunnel. But I recalled a part of the dream that was the very end. I had spent the entire day with my father.

We laughed, played, had a picnic, and talked for hours. So for some of the dream, I was my younger self and so was he.

I almost could not believe it. This entire time I thought I had only spent a few moments with him when, in fact, it felt like a lifetime of experiences in one dream. When the dream was over, and we were back in the white tunnel, my father told me that he loved me, that I was exceptional, and I am here to do great things in the world. He reminded me to be strong and that I was never alone.

Even though I still have yet to dream of my father again, recalling this dream gave me great comfort—a comfort I hope you also have experienced. It's knowing that you are here on purpose and are meant to do great things.

I believe I was finally able to connect to this message so that I can also share it with you. While I am not trained to help you recall dreams at this time, it is something I aspire to learn. But I can share with you the importance of dream work and connecting with our inner guidance.

Every night before I go to sleep, I set an intention to receive any guidance and support I may need while I am sleeping. I will invite you to try this as well, if you haven't already, and be sure to have a journal next to your bed in the morning. I often find that they tend to slip my mind if I do not write the insights down as soon as I wake up.

I find it fascinating that our ancestors utilized their dreams daily. Unfortunately, in our fast-paced society, unless we have a scary or unusual dream, we often rarely pay attention to them. Keeping a dream journal no matter how interesting or mundane your dream may seem, will leave clues and insights to guide you in your life and work. It would help if you simply started paying attention. Everyone talks about a morning ritual, but a nighttime ritual is just as important, if not more so.

Dream Work

Exercise

- One simple thing you can do is keep a dream journal;
- practice writing down your dreams this week.
- Be open to consciously and subconsciously receiving signs, guidance, and clarity.
- Set the intention before you sleep and have a journal ready in the morning.

Day 15

Personal Growth

Obstacles are opportunities for growth

When we are working toward creating something meaningful in our lives, obstacles will arise. These obstacles are not meant to be expected, but when they occur, they can cause us to doubt our path.

In 2004, I left Maui to move to New Mexico for college. It was the most significant move and decision I have ever made, but I don't remember feeling any fear. Even though it was an enormous change for me, I knew it was the right choice.

It was a major life change because I had lived in Hawaii most of my life and rarely traveled. Like most college students, it was also the first time in my life that I lived away from my mother. The difference for me was that my mother was desperately ill, and my immense guilt for leaving her in Indianapolis weighed heavily on me.

Despite these obstacles, I was determined to get my degree, make my mother proud, and do something meaningful with my life.

The weather was still warm when I arrived in Albuquerque, New Mexico, and I felt eager to settle in. However, school was starting in less than a week after my arrival, and I wanted to find a job before my first day.

My grandmother, Nana, lived in a beautiful modern townhome in the downtown area. She designed a room just for me in every house she had ever lived in since I was born. This may sound exciting, but I never got to see most of these rooms in person. Next, she moved from Illinois to Florida and lastly to New Mexico, living in multiple homes in each state.

The last time I visited her was when I was 11 and she lived in Florida. A lot had changed until I moved to New Mexico for college. I had grown up, but she expected me to be the little girl she imagined me to be.

Not too long after I arrived, she decided she would sell the townhome. I was deep into my first semester of college, and the idea of moving after I had just arrived sounded daunting. She had also promised me the townhome when I graduated from college. With this in mind, I took out large student loans, thinking I could pay them back easily because I wouldn't have to pay rent.

This all fell apart when the townhome sold quickly, and she decided to purchase a unique fixer-upper in a wrong area of town called the kill zone. I'm not making this up; I wish I was. I went from living in a gorgeous townhome to a construction zone in a matter of months. She immediately started ripping floors, tearing out windows, and gutting the bathroom. I realized later that she needed a project, but at the time, it added what felt like unnecessary stress to my first few months of college.

The renovation took an entire year, and even after it was finished, there were things she would replace. Despite it all, I stayed focused on my goal of graduating from college with my bachelor's of arts degree in graphic design. I wanted to get my dream job as soon as I graduated.

I share this story with you to avoid telling you to expect challenges. I tell you this story to encourage you to continue moving toward your dream despite the challenges that come up. While we don't want to expect that bad things will come up as we take action, we also need to be prepared if they do.

Even though that first year living in New Mexico was challenging, there were a lot of amazing things that happened. I met my husband Todd, my best friend from college Jessica, learned to snowboard, got my dream job during a recession, got my second dream job after the first dream job ended, took some fantastic trips, and ultimately accomplished what I set out to do, which got my college degree in a field that allowed me to be creative.

Day 15 Journal Prompts

How can you enhance your dream today? Make it more inspiring? Uplifting? Or concrete?

What is currently getting in the way of me taking action?

Is this a real or perceived obstacle?

What can I do today to make things easier on myself?

Where am I making things more challenging than they need to be?

How can I give myself grace while my dream unfolds?

Day 16

Resistance to the Dream

What if my dream has already been created?

As things started to unfold, this book took a few different forms. It originally started as a book about digital entrepreneurship; however, as I started to formulate the outline and my core message, I realized it was very focused on external rather than internal forces.

In writing the beginning statement, I wanted to guide you on a journey within. Connecting with yourself first would be the most beneficial. It was 2020, after all, and many of you felt lost, stuck, and unsure of which direction you wanted to take. As this resistance grew stronger, I realized I needed to do some deep dives to learn more.

I started having one-on-one conversations with you to uncover where you were, and after almost 20 deep dives I realized that many of you felt disconnected from your soul calling, off the path in your life and work, and felt a lack of clarity in what you wanted to do with your life next.

This made me realize that teaching you how to start an online business and sharing my insights about starting my service-based business as a web designer, although helpful information, was different from the information you needed at this time. And so I decided to switch genres, which felt scary because I had already announced my book and presold my idea, for which I am very grateful to my early supporters.

We always need to listen to the resistance; it doesn't necessarily mean pushing through it and doing it anyway. That the opposition is laziness or a lack of motivation. Sometimes this resistance tells us something. Sometimes it tells us to pivot, expand, and go in a different direction. This does not mean quitting, and it is OK to quit, just as long as you put something else in its place. I didn't just give up on this book because I felt resistance; I decided to really feel into what was happening and make the necessary changes.

Why did this happen? It was so I could share this insight with you now. Because we all face resistance. We start something and then question it. We start something, and it does not flow as it should. We start something, and it feels off, but we are unsure why. So it is up to us as dreamers to dive deep and get to the root of where this resistance is coming from.

For me, the resistance was coming from the fact that I felt a strong calling to write a book, but I didn't pick the right genre at first. And that is okay because I have several books in me, and the original book was not the book that was meant to come through for me at that time. The genre needed to be reworked to fit the needs of the people it needed to serve. And, yes, one of those people was me. So I am writing this book for myself and for you. I am sharing my experience with manifesting my dreams in twenty-one days because it has helped me, and I have set the intention that it will, at the very least, help one of you, if not more.

Because what is a life if we do not go after our dreams and strive to bring our creativity into the world?

So many of us are holding ourselves back, and I understand. But, birthing something is not always as easy as we might daydream about.

There were days when I wrote this book, like today, when the words flowed easily and felt magical. Then other days, I could barely meet my morning goal of writing for two hours straight. Ten minutes would go by, and I struggled to even type out a paragraph. But the more I wrote, the more I got into the daily habit, no matter what flowed out. Finally, I was committed to writing every day.

Resistance to the Dream

A note about Imposter Syndrome

For years I thought Imposter Syndrome was simply a buzzword that coaches would use on social media. Then in 2020, when the world stopped, we all had to take time to pause, reflect, and in many cases pivot—pivot our businesses, our careers, and work from home with our significant others and families.

I felt very called to reconnect with people on a deeper level to learn how they were handling this transition time and simply listen. So I scheduled 20-minute deep dives, as I called them, just to listen. I talked to those of you following my journey online—old colleagues, a few friends, and other entrepreneurs.

I heard loudly that people were feeling extremely lost, disconnected from their soul calling, and had no idea what to do next.

But the phrase I was not expecting to hear as frequently as I did in these conversations was "Imposter Syndrome." Out of my 50-plus deep dives, this word came up over 90 percent of the time.

I had no idea so many people suffered from Imposter Syndrome. They may already be successful entrepreneurs, at high levels in their careers, or stay-at-home parents. Imposter Syndrome impacts people with all different economic backgrounds, education, businesses, and employees.

You might think you are the only one suffering from Imposter Syndrome, but trust me when I say you are not alone. I strongly feel that this is an epidemic facing young and old adults.

And with the rise of social media and our constant pull to compare ourselves only makes it worse.

But what is Imposter Syndrome?

Most of us are taught to ask for permission for anything we want to do. For most of us, this permission came from our parents. For others, it was a caregiver, a teacher, or an authority figure. The intention in most cases, was to help guide us as we navigate childhood into adulthood. In a lot of instances asking permission was to keep us safe.

However, once we become adults, this permission is now up to us. We are navigating our own lives. Society expects us to know exactly what to do. But when you are so used to needing to ask for permission, it becomes challenging to make this shift when you become an adult.

Therefore you still seek consent. Permission to write that book, start that business, quit that safe job for your dream job, or get on that stage to share your truth. The challenge comes when there is someone to give you that permission. Therefore you start to wonder if your desires are valid. Because the permission comes from you.

The struggle with imposter syndrome is so common, yet people do not want to admit they feel this way for fear of judgment.

If you struggle with imposter syndrome, I want you to know you are not alone. I would encourage you to work with a trained professional to help you further.

I have come to understand this through my research and discussions with trained professionals. Disclaimer: I am not a licensed medical professional; this is not medical advice.

This has shifted in society because of a surge of people working from home, living the laptop lifestyle, and embracing the remote life. What has been my routine for so long has suddenly become the new normal for society. More people are living their dreams life than ever before.

The great resignation was the greatest awakening of our time. People are finally realizing that they are meant to do work they love. Life is meant to be experienced with joy, ease, and grace. This is the foundation for my business Work & Woo Wellness. My mission is to help as many people as I can connect back to what they are truly meant to do in life. To live up to their potential and make a true impact.

There has never been a better time to start creating meaningful work worldwide.

Day 16 Journal Prompts

Release what is no longer serving you or your dreams.

Questions to journal on:

What am I allowing into my life that no longer serves me?

How can I move away from what no longer serves me today?

What would this dream mean to you if it came to fruition?

How would this dream enhance my life for the better?

What simple actions can I take today?

Play Make-Believe and Believe

Once I realized life was happening in response to me, I started to get very clear on the life and work I wanted to create. After gaining experience working for a company, I had always dreamed of having my own business. That dream was slightly altered because my remote job allowed me to do both. The entire time I worked for Airbnb, I had my graphic and web design business on the side. I realized it was time to reimagine my side hustle and grow it into something bigger.

Believe in yourself.

Trust your own journey.

Everything in your life and business is unfolding how it is meant to.

It will be different for all of us.

But remember, we are meant to experience ups and downs.

Highs and lows are what allow us to EXPAND,

To grow,

To evolve.

If creating our dreams were easy, then we would stay stagnant.

But First, Dream Bigger

We would get bored and lose interest.

We thrive on challenges.

At our core, we love to take on BIG dreams,

So that we can accomplish great things with our lives and help those around us.

But on the challenging days, it is up to you to keep going.

Start each day by first believing in yourself.

You are capable of incredible things creative.

I believe in you.

Day 17

Confidence is Key

Get out of your comfort zone

Once I got clear on the type of work I wanted, the job I once dreaded became my dream job again. Remember when I mentioned that I moved to a new team? Well, that next year of work reminded me of why I loved Airbnb. Opportunities were coming my way like never before. I remember the day an email come through about a unique project. I immediately knew I wanted to throw my hat in the ring. My lead had the same idea because she reached out to me about it right away.

Well, that next year of work reminded me of why I loved Airbnb. Opportunities were coming my way like never before. I remember seeing an email come through about a special project. I immediately knew I wanted to throw my hat in the ring. My lead had the same idea because she reached out to me about it right away.

Manifestation is more accessible than we think. When you are clear and don't question the how or when the most amazing things will manifest in your life. I needed a change and felt the pull to grow. The result was a three-month trip to somewhere completely different from my everyday life. You can manifest anything you desire. Getting out of your comfort zone is a crucial step for growth.

If you are feeling stagnant, stuck, and unfulfilled, look at your daily routines. Which one can you change? What is no longer benefiting you? Then look at how you can do the opposite of that routine and see how you feel. It doesn't have to be a big adventure. Start simple and go from there.

The particular project was an opportunity to live and work in San Francisco for three months. Everything was paid for by the company. I was able to pick an incredible apartment that I had all to myself. All expenses were paid, including access to the Uber account. The best part was I was there to teach and speak about my experience working for the tech unicorn. It was the highlight of my career.

Three months in San Francisco taught me a lot. I'm better at public speaking than I thought. One of the biggest reasons I wanted to take this opportunity was to evolve my teaching style and public speaking. I've never feared public speaking, but I knew it was something I could improve on.

Being in the city energizes and drains me almost at the same time. City life felt incredibly overwhelming. At every corner, there is something both unexpected and predictable taking place from the cars buzzing down the street to the random homeless man asking if you can buy him a coffee. I had a fantastic time exploring, but it was also intense. It made me mindful of balancing my need for rest and adventure.

Keeping your daily rituals while traveling is vital. For example, I meditated and journaled every day while I was away. It gave me a sense of peace and helped me to feel more connected to myself. Finding a ritual you can take everywhere is crucial to staying centered.

Being open to new experiences brings in more opportunities. I met so many amazing people in San Francisco and learned so much. The benefits are still unfolding, and I'm excited about the future.

Feeling homesick is both mental and physical. I arrived in September while the weather was still warm. The first month flew by, and while I missed home before I knew it, October was here. By November rolled around, I was physically homesick, something I had never experienced before. It reminded me how truly grateful I am for my family and friends.

If people are shocked by your decisions, you're on the right path. Not one public figure we know is memorable because they played it safe. Be bold, do the unexpected, and don't hesitate to switch it up. Ninety-nine percent of the people in my life are shocked that I left Maui for so long. That's how I knew I was on the right path.

San Francisco inspires me. I received so many signs while there that told me I was meant to be there. It is incredible when you stop and pay attention to what you will learn about yourself and your journey in life.

Maui will be with me no matter where I go. Nowhere in the world feels like home the way Maui does. It is almost an indescribable feeling. It is in my heart, mind, and soul always.

But travel is good for the soul. If you get the chance to travel, take it. If you desire to go somewhere new, you can manifest it into your life. Be clear and allow it to unfold the way it is meant to.

Living and working in San Francisco for three months reminded me of why I live the life I live. While San Francisco is a fantastic city and I had such a great time, it is not the type of lifestyle I truly feel called to live. There have been times over the last several years when I wondered if I had made the right choice to move to Hawaii.

After I got my job with Airbnb as a remote employee, I realized I could live anywhere, and within six months of getting my job, I moved back to Maui with my husband, then fiancé. However, a group of remote employees decided to move to San Francisco and work from the office, or HQ as we called it. They could move to different departments and pave their way with the company.

But after my husband and daughter came to visit in October—about a month into my time there—I knew I had made the right choice. I hadn't been in San Francisco for that long and was already missing Maui. The biggest reason, or my biggest dream, for wanting to work online from home was so that I could be in control of my schedule.

I always knew I wanted to be available for my children whenever they needed me to go on field trips or events or pick them up early from school if they were sick. I did not want my children to be latchkey kids because growing up in Hawaii, I saw firsthand the impact that had on my friends. On the flip side, my mom was always home—something I was truly grateful for.

But during this time away, I missed an award ceremony for my daughter, a field trip to watch a whale, and was about to miss Halloween (my favorite holiday next to my birthday). All of this is for my dream job. Was it worth it?

For the experiences I gained in that three months, I look back and think yes and no. In the short term, missing out on important events felt hard, but it also helped me gain so much clarity. I know I could not have spent years living my life that way. I would have missed countless memorable moments if I had a traditional office job. I only had to miss three things, and it broke my heart. Sacrificing essential events for my dream job is not worth it to me. I'm happy I got a taste of that life to show that I made the best decision for myself and my family in the long run.

Making the right decision for you and your life is always best. You will never regret honoring your big dream.

Day 17 Journal Prompts

Always look within; you are being guided.

Take action on the steps right in front of you.

Don't put anything in the way.

Questions to ask yourself:

What is the path of least resistance for me today?

What do I believe is in the way of moving forward?

What new belief can I develop to move away from beliefs that are no longer serving my dream?

Day 18

Hire your Higher Self

Through mastery and long-term planning

The first time I connected with my higher self, the experience provided much peace and clarity. It was when I was searching for my purpose in life and work. During a deep meditation, I saw my higher self. She looked just like me, only a few years older. My higher self had beautiful curly hair, and gorgeous jewelry and wore a flowy dress.

She lived in a futuristic home and walked me to her office. It was modern, well-organized and filled with books. To the right side were white poster boards. She explained that she was working on a writing project. This moment inspired me to pursue my dreams of writing a book, which I had been putting on the back burner for years.

Strengthening your connection to your higher self will take time, but it is beneficial in helping you live your best life. The easiest way for you to start connecting with your higher self is by writing a letter. Once you have practiced writing to your higher self, you can begin calling to your higher self during meditation. Remember that your higher self is your best version, living in complete bliss, clarity, and ease. Imagine what you would look like, where you would live, and what you would be doing for work if there were no limitations.

At this point, you are likely on two paths with your dream. The first path takes you down the road of action while you complete the dream you started this book with and evolve it to the next level. The second path will inspire you to begin a new one. This second dream will likely take you longer than twenty-one days to achieve.

Long-term planning and the goal of mastery is focusing on anything for two to three years daily. That may be my next book. You can use the twenty-one-day guide to take you along this journey by focusing on it in this time frame. Once the first twenty-one days are complete, focus on the next. By focusing on specific time frames, two years will have passed before you know it, and you will have mastered that dream.

Use the aligned action section to help you plan your week, then turn those weeks into months and a year.

The key to this is taking action in the present moment while envisioning your higher self. Who do you want to become? What version of you has already accomplished this dream? Imagine what your higher self has already mastered in this present moment.

Set the intention to connect with your higher self through writing daily. Ask for guidance, inspiration, and support. I would date the letter to your higher self a year from today. Write in the present moment about how happy you are that your dreams have come to life. Focus on the details, your feelings, and the outcomes that have already occurred. Find a special place to keep your letter and read it in a year. You might be surprised with how many things in your letter have come to fruition.

What letter will you write to your higher self today?

Higher Self

Exercise

Date: One year from today

Dear Higher Self,

I am so happy that my dream to _____ has manifested. Thank you for helping me to _____, _____, and _____.

Love, sign your name

Day 18 Journal Prompts

Be true to yourself.

Allow ideas to flow in and out.

Take inspired action today.

Questions to journal on:

What can you try today that you haven't tried before?

Don't hold yourself back.

Your dream is waiting for you.

The Universe Always Answers You in a BIG Way.

Day 19

Answer the call

The universe always answers you in a big way

Have you ever had words speak to you so strongly that you never forget them?

The universe always answers you in a big way. For example, consider the wise words spoken to me by my mentor that I shared with you earlier in this book. Actually, her exact words were, "Wow! The universe really answered you in a big way!"

I had just manifested two months of paid time off from my job, a dream job I had loved but no longer felt in alignment with. I was suffering from burnout and unsure of what to do next. There was this strong pull toward something new, but I needed more clarity in what that something was.

It wasn't until I had an outside perspective tell me that I needed to take a break. I had never even considered taking time off, and in the world of "work hard, play harder," it seemed so simple and so complicated at the same time.

My work has always been a huge part of my life. My work was not just a job but a lifestyle, a mission, and a belief I subscribed to and still do.

And because my identity was so wrapped up in what I did, it was unclear to see them as separate.

It was a foreign concept when I realized that I needed to take a break to gain clarity. I thought because I worked online from home in Hawaii, I had work–life balance.

But I didn't. Once I realized that giving back to myself was the answer, everything shifted. Not only did I get clear on my purpose, but I realized it was right in front of me the entire time.

The universe was waiting for me to get on board with my dream. Take a break if you are being called to start something but feel stuck, trapped, or confused. Give back to yourself. Look within.

If you still feel lost, be open to supporting from those who have achieved what you desire.

The universe is here to guide you toward the people and support you seek.

All you need to do is pick up the call.

Day 19 Journal Prompts

Affirmations

I am abundant.

I am resourceful.

I am wise.

I always have more than enough.

Questions to journal on:

Do I feel abundant?

Does my dream feel abundant to me?

Am I truly stepping toward my dream with ease and grace?

In what ways can I release any heaviness around my dream to bring it closer?

Everything Unfolds the Way It Is Meant To—Always

Day 20

Divine Timing

Everything unfolds the way it is meant to.

With that being said, there is such a thing as divine timing. I do believe that everything unfolds the way it is meant to—always. And while this is a 21-day guide to support you, at the end of the 21 days you will need to make peace with where you ended up because you cannot force things to happen.

I do not believe in luck or coincidences either. Everything happens the way it is supposed to. Although you can create your reality, the time this happens is not entirely up to you. You set the intention, take action, and then let go of the outcome. This is how your dreams come to you.

This is easier said than done and will take time to master. As humans, we want to control everything and force things to happen on our timelines. But the universe does not work that way. You may be wondering why I made the guide 21 days ago.

It takes 21 days to form a habit; therefore, this daily action will help you create a dream life and work a daily habit into your life. This is what is needed to make your dream a reality.

Keep taking aligned action, get used to what that feels like, and you will have what you desire before you know it.

"But what do I do in the meantime?" you might be wondering. You continue to live your life. You continue to move forward. You cannot dwell because your dream has not manifested yet. It would be best if you continued to fill your days with the action you can take to move forward. The aligned action will always be an action you can take. And if the action you think you need to bring is outside your current ability, then you must take action to make it accessible.

Let me explain. If you desire to go to Paris and speak French but have never studied the language before, then if you purchased your ticket to Paris tomorrow, you would fall short of your desire. But if you start taking action today to begin the process of learning French, then in a few months, maybe even a year, depending on how long you study, you will be able to manifest that dream.

That is how manifestation works—you wouldn't dwell and complain and whine about how you want to go to Paris today to speak French. Instead, you would take the daily aligned action every day to learn the language so you could go to Pairs. You would build on what you learned the previous day until you were fluent.

That is the "secret" to manifestation, which, as you can see, is no secret at all. It is how most goals are achieved; it's just that we have deemed things impossible or too hard based on our beliefs. We have held ourselves back because we think it is impossible, but nothing is impossible.

Yes, miracles can happen.

Remember to underestimate the power of getting other people involved at some point to help you piece things together.

For example, you could go to Paris tomorrow with an interpreter. You aren't technically speaking French, but you could repeat what the interpreter said and learn the language that way. There are ways to make what you want to happen; you have to be creative and patiently wait.

I'll never forget when I was working for Airbnb, we had what was referred to as a World@ meeting. This meant that the entire company was invited to attend, and it was typically used to introduce new department heads. They were always virtual for me, as I worked remotely, and I would tune in as I was grabbing another cup of coffee and a snack. During this meeting, they discussed changes being made to the Singapore office, an office I had always hoped to visit but never got the chance to. And whenever we hired new people, Airbnb did this quirky thing where they asked you fun questions.

One of the fun questions in this meeting was, What was a dream you had when you were little? The woman who had just taken a prestigious job went on to explain how she had always dreamed of being a poet. She passionately spoke about her fascination with the written word. The idea of simply using her thoughts to create simple but moving art pieces brought her so much joy. Yet, as I listened to her speak, I felt so much sadness in her voice.

She had given up on this dream, even though it was what her soul was calling her to do. She didn't write on the side; she didn't plan to one day release some poems. She had completely given up on the dream to pursue a "reasonable" career in something she clearly did not love.

My heart broke for her.

I am curious to know if this woman still works for Airbnb, but I often think about her. Because she is the perfect example of so many of us who gave up on our dreams for a sensible career to live a safe and content life because this is what society demands of us. I hope this book finds its way to the dreamers who have given up.

Please don't give up. As cliché as it sounds, your dreams are waiting for you, and they want you to apply for them just as you would your mundane day job. If you have a plan that you love, wonderful. If your job is your dream, consider yourself part of the minority.

But if you still have that calling to bring another dream to life, I urge you to do it, and work at it. I would be honored to guide you on this quest to manifest it. And when you do birth this dream, I hope you'll share it with me so I can celebrate you.

I hope you will share it with the world.

There is such a thing as divine timing, and when it feels like your dream is far away, in reality, it is a lot closer than you think. Things unfold in life the way they are meant to. Sometimes it feels discouraging in the moment, but it is taking longer for reasons you are unable to fully understand. So keep taking daily aligned action. Trust the process.

Your dreams are yours for a reason.

Day 20 Journal Prompts

If your dream has manifested, have faith that it will unfold when it is meant to.

Keep taking inspired action.

Be kind to yourself.

Rest and recharge if you need to.

Create when you feel called to.

Give to receive.

In what ways can I give?

Am I able to give without expectations of receiving?

Am I truly open to receiving?

Will I openly accept help and guidance toward achieving my dream?

Day 21

Manifest Your Dreams

Hold the faith

The average person is not living their dreams, which I want to help change. Most of us dream big as children and then grow to live in the "real world," which requires us to get a real job and work in misery for forty to fifty years.

But things are quickly changing, and we are starting to awaken to a new reality. Our world has allowed us to dream even bigger, thanks to technology and the wonderful world of the internet.

Then why do so many of us still follow the conventional path—and hey, if you are happy in your career, great!

I once read somewhere that 85 percent of people loathe their jobs. That is the most depressing fact I have ever heard. We are here to dream and to dream bigger. Yet so many of us don't bring our dreams to life. I am on a mission to shift that, and I hope this book helps you to take action on your dream.

I want to reiterate that this book doesn't imply that you quit your job and be blissfully homeless. I am not encouraging you to become an entrepreneur if that does not align with you. But I encourage you to write that book, start that podcast, paint that picture, or learn that language if you have been called to do so but never did.

I truly believe I could manifest my dream life and work because I held the vision and kept the faith. I hope you will do the same.

21 Days to Dream Bigger

Journal Prompts

Always look within; you are being guided.

Take action on the steps right in front of you.

Don't put anything in the way.

Questions to journal on:

What is the path of least resistance for me today?

What do I believe is in the way of moving forward?

What new belief can I develop to move away from the belief that is no longer serving my dream?

Manifested my way home to Maui

One day I realized that the dream I had set when I was 16 years old had manifested. At the time, I had no idea what manifestation was. I had a vision for how I wanted my life to be. I now realize I created my life; it did not just happen.

In 2012, almost seven months after moving back home to Maui, I married my best friend. Planning out a wedding was a manifestation as we searched for a venue. My maid of honor, Lindsay, found the magical spot on the beautiful Northshore cliffs. When we visited it, the owner seemed suspicious, and we quickly decided it wasn't the right spot.

I was about to think we would never find the perfect venue. We had already sent out our save-the-date notes, and our guests were starting to make travel plans. I decided to stop searching and focus on the things I could take action on.

The biggest thing I needed to figure out next to the venue was finding an Airbnb for our wedding party to stay at. I started looking for listings in the up-country Maui area because I knew I wanted to get married somewhere close to Makawao, where I grew up.

After scrolling through countless options, I found an Airbnb called Charming Unique Log House Retreat. The photo showed a beautiful willow tree in the front yard, and it reminded me of something from a fairy tale. It looked perfect.

I contacted the host, Eve, to see if she would be open to showing me the listing before I booked. I explained that the listing would be for my wedding party and wanted to ensure it was the right fit. She kindly agreed because I lived only ten minutes away. The location was ideal!

We agreed to meet later that week, and as we walked around the property, she explained that she had just listed the house on Airbnb. If I decided to book it, I would be her first guest. It all felt too good to be true, and then she asked the winning question: "So, where are you getting married?". My fiancé and I looked at each other. "Well, we don't exactly have a venue yet."

At this point, the wedding was less than six months away, and Eve looked at us, slightly concerned. Then she said, "Well, you know we also host weddings here?" I almost fell over, and as she walked us down to the property where she performed weddings as the officiant, she asked if we had ever heard of a labyrinth wedding.

Next door to the Airbnb was a giant greenhouse filled with gorgeous plants, water features, and abundant flowers. The property used to be called Maliko Farms, but Eve had transformed it into the Sacred Garden of Maliko. We walked to the back of the greenhouse, and this large circle rock formation was completely surrounded by gorgeous tall trees. Behind it was a lovely stream that added a subtle sound of trickling water.

It was not only magical but beyond any wedding venue I could have ever imagined.

Eve finished explaining the symbolism of a labyrinth ceremony and how it was about starting our life together as one. We each entered the labyrinth separately and were now living our life together when we walked out. Before she could even ask us if we needed to think about it, we said yes.

My husband, Todd, and I were married on October 28, 2012, in the labyrinth, surrounded by family and friends.

I often wander around the sacred labyrinth with our daughter. She loves to hear how we met and about our wedding day. I try to visit at least once a month to reflect and release anything weighing me down. This particular day it was raining off and on, which I always find so relaxing.

I found a little spot in the garden with some art supplies. There was an adult coloring book filled with amazing quotes, and this one by Buddha caught my eye. We often carry the weight of past experiences, severely limiting us from moving forward. I'm sharing this as a reminder to focus on what makes you happy, excites you, and lights you up. This will guide you into bringing what you truly desire into your life. I will remember to do the same.

I am truly grateful for the life I am living now, and I truly believe that my dreaming bigger is what got me here.

Today is the last day of the journaling exercise. I sincerely hope you have found it beneficial. However, it is important to look back on the last 21 days.

Keep going, even if your dream has not manifested yet. Keep taking daily aligned action.

Now that you have formed the habit of what it feels like to listen to your inspired ideas allow them to continue to move you forward once this dream manifests.

Day 21 Journal Prompts

Hold the vision; trust the process.

Look back on the last 21 days.

What actions, thoughts, words, and stories have benefited the dream the most?

Looking ahead to the next 21 days, what habits, intentions, and actions will you continue to take?

Sitting here today, in the present moment, what can you step into that will best serve your dream?

Always Remember That No One Can Ever Take Away Your Dreams. Your Dreams Are Yours for a Reason.

Dear Dreamer,

Remember, building anything takes time, effort, and work. Starting with a solid foundation in self-love and self-care is paramount to making it through the ups and downs of life and work.

Positive affirmations are one key ritual I do throughout my day. It is easy to overlook how we talk to ourselves. But it is so imperative to keep our self-talk as beautiful as possible.

It sets us up to take action on whatever we wish to create in this world.

I hope this book helps you create the rituals needed to help you bring many BIG dreams into your life.

Always be kind to yourself, Dreamer.

Lots of love,

Nadia

Guided Meditations

By Nadia Mau Bernardy | nadiabernardy.com

Guided Meditations

Meditate Daily; Change Your Life

People often tell me that they struggle to meditate. You may be one of those people who can't seem to sit still and clear your mind. As a multi-passionate person with too many ideas, I struggle to meditate.

It wasn't until I took a workshop in San Francisco for a work trip that I succeeded with this practice. You can probably relate to this, but I always thought meditation was about clearing your mind and not thinking about anything. To sit in a state of true relaxation with a clear and empty mind. This has probably felt nearly impossible if you are like me and have many ideas.

What I learned during this meditation workshop, however, was that it was not about forcing your mind to go completely blank. In fact, it was the complete opposite. Meditation is a practice for you to observe your thoughts. Pay attention to what is naturally coming to mind, and do not trying to make yourself not think of anything.

I like to think of my thoughts as waves of inspiration. Sometimes they are profound ideas, and sometimes I'm just thinking about how I need to eat something. It does not matter how enlightened or how mundane, silly, or odd your thoughts are. The point is to observe them.

Let your thoughts flow in and out like waves gently rolling up the beach and then back out again. Once you can pay attention to your ideas and observe them, you will start to be able to meditate for longer periods.

When I first started meditating, I could only last five minutes or so, then if I was really trying. But after using guided meditations, I can now deliberate on my own for about 20 to 30 minutes and up to an hour with guided meditation.

After taking the meditation workshop in San Francisco, I found another guided meditation class here in Maui at the Sacred Garden of Maliko. This is one of my favorite places on the island, not only because I was married there in the labyrinth by the owner but because I feel immediately at peace every time I step foot in this gorgeous place.

Anytime I think conflicted or need to work through my thoughts, I go here and walk the labyrinth—often with my daughter, who loves this sacred place almost as much as I do.

I find that getting out in nature is also a way to help me meditate. Meditation does not necessarily mean sitting with your eyes closed, if this feels too hard. Instead, try walking outdoors or at your favorite place and just let your thoughts wander.

Now that I have grasped meditation, I aim to share this practice with you. The intention is to continue this practice by not rushing it but gently guiding yourself toward meditating for even longer. I included some guided meditations in the book to help you start this beneficial practice.

Like anything else, it is a practice you learn to develop over time. It is not about forcing yourself to meditate for twenty minutes a day. It is about choosing a time in the morning, evening, or day when you can sit and be with yourself.

I also want to note that you don't necessarily need to sit quietly and close your eyes. Mediate in a way that makes sense for you rather than sitting in your favorite chair, lying on your bed, or finding a place outside. Sometimes I sit with my eyes open and look out into the trees on my lanai.

Do what works for you until it becomes second nature. The divine feminine, which can apply to both women and men, asks us to master skills over the long term. So focus on this daily for as long as necessary before it becomes second nature.

I don't even think about meditating daily anymore; I do. Sometimes I meditate in the morning, but sometimes I don't think about it until later. So you can make this a practice that makes sense for you and your life.

The benefits of mediation are endless, and I have included some meditations that I created specifically to go along with the journal prompts in the book. My hope is that by starting with a guide, you can see what works for you.

The mediations included in this book are very intentional and meant to help you along your soul-led journey. The grounding meditation is very powerful, and I recommend doing it a few times a week. I typically do this meditation when I am struggling to stay focused. So again, find what works for you, but if you are new to meditation, I want to advise you to have patience with grounding.

Prepare yourself and your space, as you want to feel comfortable while meditating. I would suggest having a journal for you to use when you are done. This is a mediation you want to plan to do. Pick a time when you can be relaxed and not disturbed.

I first did this meditation as a guided meditation with my spiritual business coach, and it brought me so much profound insight that I wanted to put it in this book. It was when I felt disconnected from myself, my soul calling, and was unclear on what I wanted to do with my life and work.

This was a feeling I had never experienced before, and this mediation helped me gain clarity. One of the biggest revelations I had was the fact that I am a writer. I had put it on the back burner for so long for so many reasons. And here it reminded me that I needed to focus on this practice, like meditation. I write every day, primarily through journaling. It inspired me to start writing this book.

I hope the guided meditations will inspire you to find that dream you have been putting on the back burner.

Three Meditation Insights

Meditate Daily; Change Your Life

Every new moon, I visit the labyrinth at the Sacred Garden of Maliko, which I often share on my Instagram Stories @nadiamaubernardy, to meditate and set my monthly intention. Mediation has been immensely beneficial for me when starting my online business. It helps me to stay clear throughout my day, and no matter how hectic things get, I can remain focused. I wanted to share three insights that have helped me in practicing meditation:

1. Try meditating first thing in the morning; it is easier in a sleepy state.
2. Let your thoughts float in and out. I always thought you had to empty your mind, but it is about acknowledging the ideas that come to you and releasing them.
3. A guided meditation class is great for getting started. Find a class locally or look for a mediation online, such as nadiabernardy.com

Cosmic Meets Earth Grounding Meditation

Use it anytime you feel drained and disconnected.

Get into a comfortable seated position. Put your feet on the floor or lie down if your energy has been drained. Take a deep breath, and focus on releasing everything from your day. Then, take another deep breath and close your eyes, focusing on releasing everything from your day, and take another deep breath.

Now imagine at the base of your spine from your root chakra that, there is a grounding cord. This cord can look however you imagine it to look. This cord can be a vine with beautiful flowers, it can be gold and shiny, it can be made out of candy, or it can be rainbow-colored.

Imagine this cord is attached to the base of your spine and allow it to flow down to the floor you are sitting on. Imagine it flowing through the floor and through the ground, and it reaches the dirt, the rocks. Imagine it going farther and farther down into the earth until it reaches the center of the earth's core.

Imagine the cord is wrapping around the core of the earth. Even notice a little tug as it secures itself to the earth's core. You are now connected to Mother Earth, to all her beauty, all the richness she has to offer, and all her support.

Now that you are connected to the earth, imagine a bright golden sun above the top of your head. It's beautiful, bright, golden sparkling, and glowing. This sun is infusing a light that is comforting and warm.

Think about all the energy you released during this week while running errands, working, driving, or taking care of your loved ones. Imagine that all the energy you have used this week connecting with other people, creating new projects, and experiencing new things is returning to you. Imagine all this energy. Every last bit is now being pulled back into the bright golden sun above your head.

You may see this energy as white light coming back towards you or as golden sparks. However, your energy looks like to you; whatever color you imagine, it is all being pulled back into the sun.

Once all your energy from the week has been pulled back into the sun, imagine that this sun bursts, and all the beautiful light. The sparkly light, the white light, the golden shimmery is pouring down from the top of your head across your face, neck, shoulders, arms, and body to your feet. And you feel amazing, comforted, supported, replenished, energized, happy, and secure.

Imagine your whole body glowing with this beautiful light. Sit with the feeling of being whole again, and let the sense of recharge fill up your entire body.

Now that this light is covering you and you have all your energy back from the week, I want you to focus on a light above your head. This light flows up, up high into the sky, higher than you can imagine. There is a constant stream of this white light from the top of your head to the sky.

This light then starts to flow down your face, past your shoulders, and down your body. Remember your connection to your grounding cord as this light is coming down. Imagine robust and comforting light from your grounding cord now meeting this white light from the sky.

This earth energy and cosmic light energy are now bleeding together and flowing through your body. Replenishing all your energy and flowing through your waist, down your legs, all the way down to your feet, and back up again. It flows through your body up to your shoulders, to the top of your head and back down again.

As this energy flows through your body, imagine that it is releasing any tension you may be feeling, any stress you have, all the thoughts that are keeping you down, any situation during the week that weighed you down, anything that made you feel upset is all being moved through your body and is being released with this energy.

This weight is no longer serving you; it is time to release it. Think of all this heaviness being released so you can feel aligned, uplifted, calm, and at peace.

Now that this energy moves, the last little bit of stagnant energy that is no longer serving you is going back up to the sky, and the earth energy is clearing out all the way back out of the grounding cord. You are releasing your connection to the earth's core and letting go of your grounding cord. You still feel secure, safe, and contained.

Once your grounding cord has been released, you can open your eyes.

The Cosmic Meets Earth Grounding Meditation is beneficial to use at least once a week or anytime you feel drained or tired.

Listen to the audio version of this meditation at nadiabernardy.com/grounding

Perfect Day Meditation

Use with the Perfect Day Exercise

Sit in a comfortable upright position. Place your hands on your lap. Legs relaxed, and gently close your eyes.

Take slow breaths and begin to picture a quiet, still morning. You are in a beautiful field, the sun is warm on your face, there is a slight breeze, and you feel completely relaxed.

You start slowly walking, picking flowers until you find a path. There are tall trees as far down the path as you can see. You hear birds chirping faintly in the distance. You start slowly walking down the trail.

As you approach the path's end, you see a picnic table. There is an array of art supplies, and you feel called to create. You sit down and start selecting colors.

You see gorgeous blues, golden yellows, greens, and purples. You are expressing how you want to show up in the world through your creativity. How you wish to give back to others. How you wish to give back to yourself.

The things you truly wish to accomplish. The places you desire to see. You are creating your perfect day. The time is slowly passing, and you feel your creation is complete.

You stand up and start walking back to the tall trees. You see another path, and as you enter, the wind picks up. You see the clouds moving in the sky. The day is coming to a close.

You come to the end of the path and are back to the open field. You look out to see the sunset clouds with light pinks and soft oranges. You are instantly filled with happiness.

Your perfect day was everything you hoped it would be. As you reminisce about your day, you focus back on your breath. Breathing in and out slowly, in and out, in and out.

And when you are ready, you start to wiggle your toes. Your fingers move slowly. Focusing on your breath, you slowly open your eyes.

Listen to the audio version of this meditation at nadiabernardy.com/perfectday

Aura Meditation

To boost your confidence

Visualize your auric field, and play around with different colors and textures. Your Aura is whatever color resonates with you the most. See it as a beautiful light bubble surrounding your entire body.

Your Aura can be however you imagine it to be. Glowing brightly, sparkling like glitter, calm, and smooth. The image that comes to mind first is the right one; trust that you have the perfect Aura.

Now imagine that your Aura surrounds your entire body.

If you feel reserved, experiment with expanding your Aura around your entire body.

If you are feeling open, bring your Aura closer to you.

Before you leave your house, imagine that your Aura is protecting you and your energy. Keeping you safe, comfortable, and happy.

Affirmations to strengthen your Aura:

My Aura is strong and supports all my dreams. I am the Divine having a human experience. I am guided by my own inner wisdom.

Listen to the audio version of this meditation at nadiabernardy.com/aura

Special Thank You

Forever Grateful

Without you, I could not have worked with my publisher to make this dream book a reality. I am truly thankful to my Super Supporters who preordered my book when it was simply an inspired idea. I am forever grateful for your kindness. I am forever grateful that you believed in this project when it was an inspired idea. Lots of Aloha, Nadia

Aron Just preordered the book. More than happy to support Nadia in the journey that she is so passionate about. She is one of the kindest people in this world and deserves this success. Can't wait to see her book being sold at Barnes and Noble. Wishing her all the best and good luck with her book.

Mint Proud of you, Nadia!!! ❤

Nicole, Got my copy! Good luck!

Fran, Keep on being amazing! ❤

Genesis, What an exciting project! Wishing you all the success in the world.

Liza

Joe

Lavina

Acknowledgments

Mahalo and Gratitude

Thank you to my husband, Todd, for supporting my dream of living on Maui and raising our incredible daughter. I could not have manifested my dream life and business without you. To my amazing daughter, Pania, for being my biggest fan. You inspire me daily, and being your mama has been my greatest gift.

To my Indy family Aunt Joanne, Kim, Imani, Immanuel, Marcus, Ellis, Jay, Charles, and Corey. I love you all more than you know. Even though we live far apart, I can feel your love; it means the world to me.

To my in-laws, Russ and Trish Bernardy, who have always made me feel like family. We've had so many fun times, and I look forward to our next Bernardy Party.

To my incredible godmother, Mary. Thank you for your constant support. To Steve and Laura, I am very grateful that we reconnected.

To my Hanai Maui Ohana and Friends

A special acknowledgment to my late parents.

This book was inspired by my mother's perseverance to go after her biggest dream, to be an artist, raise me in Hawaii, and live the life she felt truly called to live. I love you, Mommy Max. To my late father, I hope to reconnect with you in my dreams again.

To all of my friends and family around the globe.

I love you ALL.

Acknowledgments

Mahalo and Gratitude

Lastly but certainly not least to, all the Dreamers who support my work online by following me on social media, subscribing to my YouTube channel, listening to my podcast, enrolling in my courses, and working with me as your mentor.

I see all your beautiful comments and read every message. I am inspired by your dedication to dreaming BIGGER.

Thank you for your support while I created my dreams. I hope this book inspired you to go after your dreams too.

-Lots of Aloha

Nadia

Testimonials

"Thank you for helping us build Airbnb."

"Joe, Nate, and I want to thank you for being part of Airbnb and helping build Airbnb as one of our early employees. Few will understand just how different it was back then—it wasn't as obvious we would be successful, there were fewer processes, and we all had to step up at a frantic pace. Thank you for helping us build Airbnb. Thank you for carrying the culture forward. And thank you for being a great example for all those who joined after you."

—Airbnb Founders: Brian, Joe, and Nate

"Nadia is a constant professional."

I have worked with Nadia for over ten years, and the experience has always been easy and fun. Nadia is a constant professional and can be relied on for anything she says she will help. I cannot express how highly I would recommend her and her services!

—ABQ-Live the Magazine CEO/Founder:

Josh Vandlandingham

From Soul Calling to Soulfulpreneur

Aloha, Dreamer,

If, after reading this book, you feel called to create your soul-led business and are looking for support, then I would invite you to apply for the SOUL STARTUP, Business, and Branding Immersion.

This is my signature program designed to help you take the principles learned in this book and apply them to your dream online business, personal brand, and spiritual development journey.

If this program sounds right for you, to learn more, visit:

www.nadiabernardy.com/startup

It would be an honor to work with you and help you bring your inspired ideas to life.

-Nadia

Offerings and Resources

Visit nadiabernardy.com

Tune into the podcast:
nadiabernardy.com/podcast

Meditation Links:
nadiabernardy.com/grounding
nadiabernardy.com/perfectday
nadiabernardy.com/aura

E-Journal Links:
nadiabernardy.com/gratitude
nadiabernardy.com/selftalk

Decoding Your Birthday, Numerology 101 Workshop:
nadiabernardy.com/birthday

Follow and connect on social media:
https://www.youtube.com/c/nadiabernardy
https://www.instagram.com/nadiamaubernardy/
https://www.facebook.com/nadiamaubernardy

Email Nadia:
aloha@nadiabernardy.com

Affiliates and Product Suggestions

Book mentioned:
StrengthsFinder 2.0 by Tom Rath
The Hero's Journey by Joseph Campbell

Online Business Tools:
Siteground Web Hosting: https://www.siteground.com/recommended?referrer_id=117857

Thrive Themes:
https://thrivethemes.com/affiliates/ref.php?id=11560

Aweber Email:
https://workandwoo.aweber.com

Creative Market:
https://creativemarket.com/?u=wanderfulmama

Airbnb:
https://www.airbnb.com/c/nbernardy?s=3&i=1
Beauty: https://www.thegoldensecrets.com/

For 10% off use code nadia10

Please note that some of these links are affiliates, which means I will receive a credit if you sign up.

About the Author

Nadia Mau Bernardy a spiritual entrepreneur, intuitive business mentor and author based in Maui, Hawaii. Nadia graduated with a bachelor of arts degree in graphic design, web design, and marketing from the South West University of Visual Arts in Albuquerque, New Mexico, in December of 2007.

After graduating, she helped grow an unknown tech startup into a $75 billion international brand, all while working from her laptop in Hawaii. Nadia now helps women and men go from career burnout to soul-led lifestyles through life coaching, online courses, and workshops.

When she is not coaching, Nadia loves to explore her island home with her husband and daughter

Connect with Nadia:

www.nadiabernardy.com

www.ingramcontent.com/pod-product-compliance
Lightning Source LLC
Chambersburg PA
CBHW060528080526
44586CB00012B/668